VersaCharm Classic Collection

THE BRAVEST WOMEN

True Stories that Inspired Generations

Louise Creighton

VCB

**VersaCharm
Books**

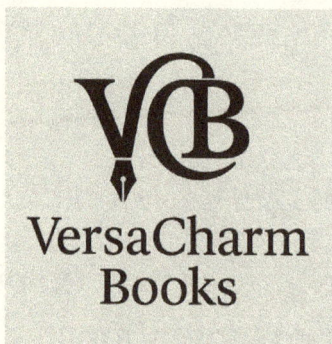

Email: contact@versacharm.com
Website: versacharm.com

Contents

Louise Creighton – The Quiet Light

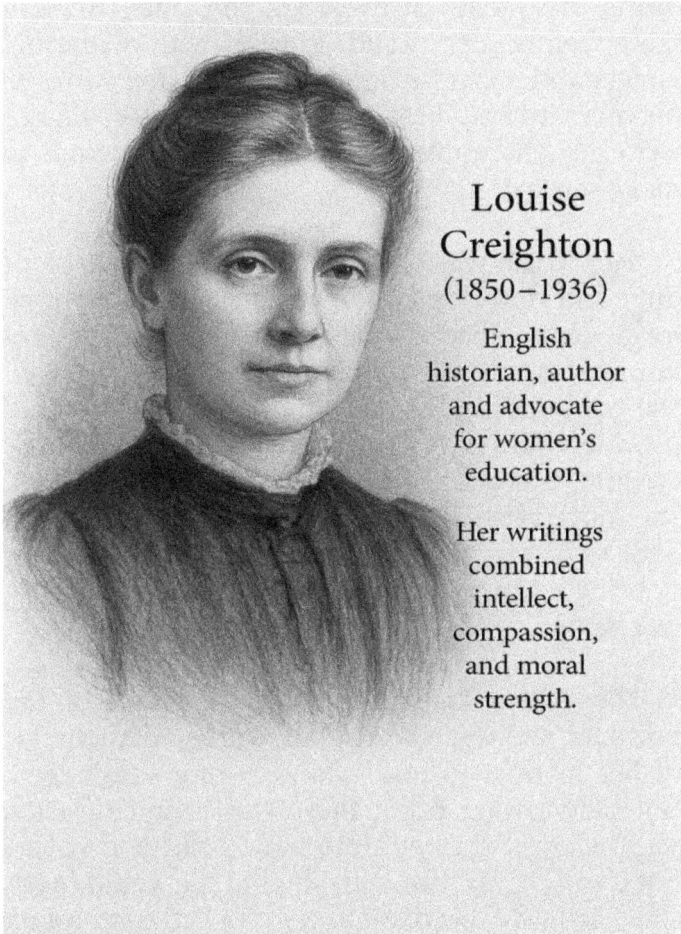

Louise Creighton
(1850–1936)

English historian, author and advocate for women's education.

Her writings combined intellect, compassion, and moral strength.

In the still hush of a late Victorian morning, when London's fog had not yet lifted and the carriages murmured faintly in the street, a woman sat at her writing desk. She was not seeking fame or recognition. Her hands, pale and graceful, rested on the edge of a stack of papers—letters, drafts, fragments of lives. On the small wooden table before her stood a vase with withering violets and a candle, its flame trembling with the movement of her breath. Louise Creighton did not write for the applause of her age; she wrote to make sense of it.

Her world was one of measured politeness, of duty and devotion, where women were expected to be gentle shadows beside their husbands. Yet Louise's mind was quietly radiant. Born in 1850, she grew up in an England tightening the corset of propriety around its daughters, yet cautiously opening the doors of education. From the start, she moved between obedience and thought, faith and reason, the heart and the intellect. Her upbringing was simple, but her hunger for books was vast.

Those who knew her in youth spoke of her poise, of the way she listened rather than spoke, of her instinct to understand before she judged. But behind that calm, there was a fierce clarity. She believed that education was not a privilege but a calling. And though she did not yet know it, she would become one of those quiet revolutionaries who changed the world not by shouting, but by writing gently and truly.

In those years, England was a nation trembling on the edge of modernity. The empire was at its height, the poor were many, and women were voiceless in politics. Yet in parlors and in classrooms, questions began to stir about morality, poverty, and the soul of the nation. Louise would soon find herself at the center of that moral awakening, guided not by ambition, but by conscience.

••• ✦ •••

Louise Elizabeth Hope, as she was born, was educated in a time when the word *education* meant something very different for girls. To be well-educated meant to be fluent in charm, in patience, and in silence. But Louise's curiosity was not ornamental. She devoured history, theology, and literature with equal hunger. Her teachers recognized in her a composure that did not come from meekness but from thought. She had, as one contemporary said, the dignity of a mind at work.

That quiet independence was what first drew Mandell Creighton to her, a young man of ideas, a scholar of history, later to become the Bishop of London. When they met, there was no thunderclap of romance, only an immediate meeting of minds. He saw in her what few men of his age dared to value: a woman whose intellect was not in competition with his, but in harmony. Their marriage was not a union of convenience, but of conscience. Together, they built a life of thought and faith. Their home was filled with books and the laughter of their children, but also with endless discussion about ethics, duty, and the role of the Church in a changing world.

Mandell's career as a clergyman exposed them to both the grandeur and the contradictions of Victorian religion. Louise, with her grounded sense of truth, became his moral compass. She wrote first as a companion to his work, but soon, her voice began to separate, to grow into something unmistakably her own. She observed the world around her, the sacrifices of women, the silent courage of mothers and teachers, the quiet suffering that went unrecorded, and she began to write about them. Not with pity, but with reverence.

Her writing was not political in form, but deeply political in spirit. "I do not wish to fight," she once wrote, "only to remind the world that the strongest souls often speak softly."

••• ✦ •••

Life beside Mandell brought Louise into the quiet center of English intellectual life, though she never wore it as an honor. She preferred the study to the stage, the letter to the speech, the thought to the argument. Yet her influence spread silently, like light through a half-drawn curtain. Guests who entered their home in Oxford or later in

London would often remark on the calm of the place. Books lined the walls from floor to ceiling, and on the table near the hearth there were always fresh pages covered in her delicate handwriting. She wrote as one breathes: constantly, naturally, without the need for display.

Motherhood did not erase her intellect; it deepened it. Surrounded by her seven children, she learned to see patience not as resignation but as strength. The rhythm of her life followed that of the house itself: mornings filled with lessons and letters, afternoons with visits and parish work, evenings returning to the desk. Her discipline was quiet and absolute. She seemed to understand that the only way to keep her mind alive was to feed it daily, no matter how little time remained after the duties of the day.

There were days of exhaustion, of course, days when the ink dried in the pen and the world outside her window felt too heavy. But she believed in persistence, in the holiness of routine. Every sentence she shaped was an act of faith in the worth of human thought. Her journals from those years show no bitterness, no lamentation for opportunities lost. Instead, they reveal a woman who believed that truth was not confined to universities or pulpits, but could live in a kitchen, in a letter, in the voice of a mother telling her child about courage.

Her faith was not the narrow faith of dogma, but a broad trust in goodness. While Mandell argued theology in the halls of Cambridge, Louise practiced it in life. She believed that to teach a child to think kindly was holier than to make him memorize verses. Her religion was not obedience; it was clarity, compassion, and the refusal to look away from suffering.

As the years passed, the boundaries of her world widened. She read of reform movements in America, of suffragists demanding the vote, of new schools for girls being built in the English countryside. The age was changing, and she, though cautious by temperament, felt a stirring in her heart. She began to write about women—not as figures of virtue or vice, but as minds, as moral beings whose choices shaped the world as surely as those of men.

From that quiet conviction grew the idea for the book that would outlive her. It came not from ambition but from observation. She had met too many women whose courage went unnamed, whose work was dismissed as duty rather than destiny. History, she thought, was incomplete; it recorded crowns and parliaments but not the quiet endurance that sustained them. She

6

decided, with the humility of someone who expects no reward, to fill that absence with stories.

In the evenings, when the children slept and the lamps burned low, she would open her notebooks and begin to trace the outlines of other lives. Queens and saints, reformers and writers—women who had borne the weight of their time and still found a way to act with grace. She read their letters, their confessions, their final words. Then she rewrote them, not as lessons but as mirrors, so that those who read might glimpse the same strength within themselves.

When *Some Famous Women* began to take form, she knew it would never be a grand book. It was simple by intention, written for the hearts of young readers. She wanted her daughters, and all daughters, to see that goodness was not frailty and that heroism did not always come with triumph. In each story she placed a small light, the same steady glow that guided her through her own life.

Her prose was tender and unhurried, a quiet conversation across time. She refused melodrama; she sought truth. The book spoke of women who had failed as often as they had succeeded, but whose failure had the dignity of effort. To read it was to feel the hush of reverence, the pause between thought and prayer. And when it was published, the response was small but sincere. A few reviewers noticed its grace; teachers passed it on to their pupils; mothers kept it on bedside tables. It was never loud enough to echo, but it never truly faded either.

Those who visited Louise in those years found her surrounded by calm. Her husband's health was failing, and her own days were heavy with care, yet she remained unshaken. Her letters from that period speak of gratitude more than grief. "There is work enough in kindness," she wrote once, "to keep a heart from breaking."

••• ✧ •••

After her husband's passing, the house grew quieter, but not lifeless. Louise kept the rhythm of her days, as though to honor the memory of all they had built together. Morning light fell across the same desk where they had once planned sermons and essays, and though one chair now stood empty, the habit of thought remained. She did not mourn in public; grief for her was a private devotion, something offered silently to the air, as if words might disturb the peace of his rest.

In those solitary years she returned again to writing, not out of ambition but out of need. Her pen became a companion, the ink a form of prayer. The world around her was changing quickly now: the first machines roared through the streets, women marched in protest, and the old manners of England began to loosen. Yet she herself did not grow bitter or fearful. She watched with quiet pride as the things she had long believed—the worth of women's education, the dignity of moral work, the beauty of thought— began to take root in the world beyond her own home.

Her letters from that time are tender and clear, free of complaint. She writes of the garden, of her daughters' laughter, of the sound of rain on the glass when she reads. She speaks of books as though they were living friends, of silence as a teacher. There is no sense of regret in her words, only an awareness of how precious it is to have lived a thoughtful life.

Those who knew her then described her as "quietly radiant." Visitors would find her sitting by the fire, her hands folded in her lap, her gaze turned toward the window as if she were still listening for someone who had stepped just beyond the room. She asked little of the world, except that it remain kind.

When the young women of her parish came to seek her advice, she never lectured. She would pour the tea, listen patiently, and answer in the simplest way possible: "Do good carefully." It was a phrase that stayed with many of them, a seed of wisdom planted without ceremony. Her gentleness had weight.

Louise Creighton's later years passed without great events, but they were full of meaning. She continued to write, to mentor, to believe in the quiet endurance of decency. When she spoke of history, it was never as a sequence of wars or kings, but as a tapestry woven from patience and mercy. "We are all," she once wrote, "the keepers of one another's courage."

By the time she died in 1936, the world had moved far from the one she was born into. There were automobiles now instead of carriages, new voices shouting for freedom, new doubts replacing old certainties. Yet her ideas, though never loud, had endured. The women she wrote for had become readers, teachers, reformers, citizens. The moral fabric she had trusted still held, though stretched thin.

Her home was modest, her possessions few. But on the desk, beside the worn pen and a small bowl of violets, there remained a single notebook—its pages filled with reflections written in her careful hand. The last entry was dated a few months before her death: *"Light does not need to dazzle. It only needs to remain."*

Those words could have been her epitaph.

Today, when her name appears, it is often in small type, in the footnotes of history. But to read her work is to rediscover the stillness at the heart of thought. She was a woman of faith, not in doctrine but in goodness; a woman of letters, not for acclaim but for truth. In her life there was no spectacle, no grand rebellion—only the steadfast belief that what is right and tender and kind will outlast everything that is not.

Louise Creighton's legacy is not measured in fame, but in influence that cannot be seen. It is in the classrooms where girls study freely, in the books that speak of women as thinkers, in the quiet resolve of every person who believes that decency is still a force of change. Her light was never meant to blind; it was meant to guide. And it still does.

Author's Preface (1909)

By Louise Creighton

In this little book I am going to tell you about some of the women who have been famous in the past. There are perhaps many names more famous than those I have chosen, but it was not always the best women who were the most talked about. In the past it was seldom that any woman, who was not a royal lady or some great aristocrat, became known to the world. In the early days of Christianity, many women suffered bravely for their faith, and later in the convents there were studious nuns who became known for their learning. In the account of St. Hilda you will read of one of the most famous of these. But most women were busy in keeping their houses, and had to do many things which no woman would dream of doing now. Cloth and linen had to be woven at home, simple medicines and ointments were made by the great ladies, who had often to act as doctors as well as nurses. Only few women had any book learning, and it was long before it was thought desirable for a woman to learn to write. When good schools were started for boys, few people thought it desirable to do anything for the education of girls. It was not till the nineteenth century that a change began, and that people as a rule began to think that, as girls had minds as well as boys, it was as well to give them the chance of learning. When you read about Mrs. Somerville, you will see how great was the change in her lifetime. No one troubled to teach her when she was a child, but before her death the first colleges for women were founded at Cambridge.

Joan of Kent is an example of the aimless life led by a great lady in the Middle Ages who was kindly and beloved, but did not know how to make her life of use to others. Margaret Beaumont was also a great lady and might have spent her days in pleasure, but the experiences of her life made her serious, and she used her life and her money in the service of others. Since their day, there have been many great ladies who have been like one or other of these two.

The first way in which women who had no great position in the world made themselves famous was by their care for the poor and the suffering. What such women could do, and there have been very many of them, is seen in the lives of Elizabeth Fry, Sister Dora, and Florence Nightingale. Other women have given their lives to sharing the sorrows and anxieties of their husbands, and by their love and devotion have been their greatest help in difficult times. These are seldom known to fame, but we see examples of them in Lady Rachel Howard and Lady Inglis. But whilst most women would always choose a quiet home life there are others, of whom Mrs. Bishop is an example, who are filled with the spirit of adventure, and like to face difficulties and to see new things. It is not possible in one small book to give examples of all the different kinds of women who have lived for the service of others. I should like to have told you something about the women doctors, the great women teachers, the women writers and novelists. From all their lives you would learn one lesson which is set forth clearly in the life of Queen Victoria. Nothing worth doing is done without a great deal of trouble. The ruler of a great empire has to work as hard as any girl in a factory, and Queen Victoria is known as a great queen, not because she had talents above other women, but simply because she set herself to do her duty in the position in which God had placed her. In that we can all imitate her.

But what shall I say about the one woman in our book who is not English, the Maid of France? She seems to me to stand apart from all other women, like a beautiful vision for our delight and reverence. But she is like all other good women in this that she did the thing that lay before her. Without fear, in perfect simplicity, she took up the task to which she felt she was called, and went straight on without looking back, even to death.

We do not know what work may be asked from women in the future, but the same spirit will still be needed—the capacity to take trouble, the readiness to do difficult things when duty calls, and the gentle spirit of love which, in spite of all her learning, made Mrs. Somerville a better wife and mother than most even of those who have devoted themselves entirely to their domestic duties.

••• ✧ •••

CHAPTER I

Saint Hilda

··· ✧ ···

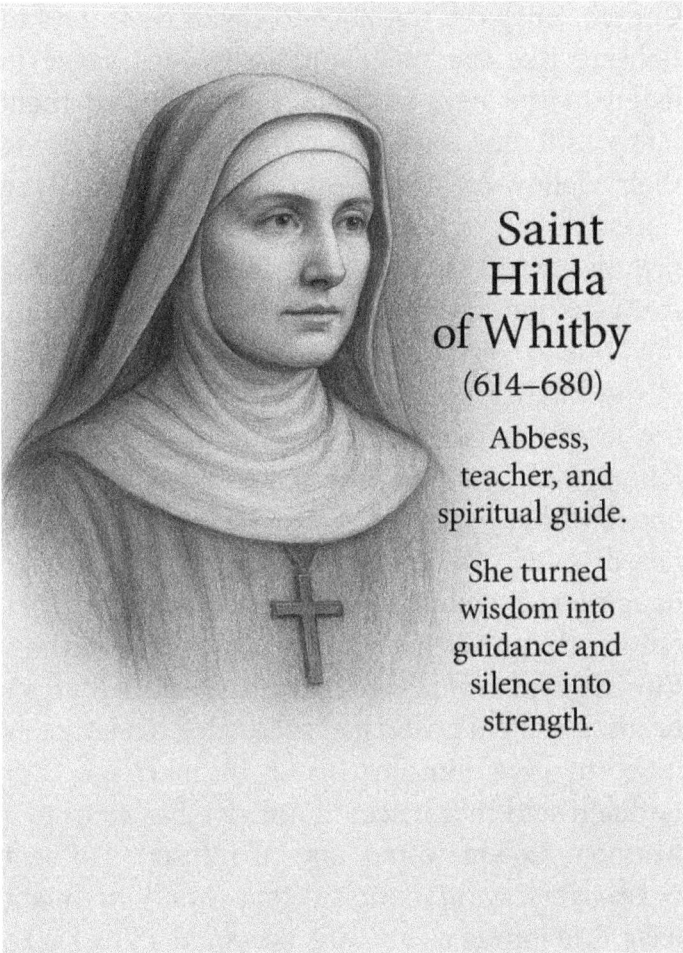

Saint
Hilda
of Whitby
(614–680)

Abbess,
teacher, and
spiritual guide.

She turned
wisdom into
guidance and
silence into
strength.

Amongst our forefathers, the wild German tribes who conquered Britain and made it England, women had always held an honourable place. This made it possible for them, in the days when the Christian faith was first preached in England, to do a great deal to help the work of the Church. They did not have to spend their days in fighting like the men, and they were eager to listen to the new teaching which showed them many different ways of serving God and helping their fellow-creatures. Probably it was the Christian wife of Ethelbert, King of Kent, a French princess, who helped to make him willing to listen to Augustine, the missionary sent from Rome by the Pope to convert the English. Kent was the first of the English kingdoms to become Christian. In the northern part of England there was a great king called Edwin, who ruled over Northumbria and had his capital at York. He seems to have heard much in praise of one of Ethelbert's daughters, Ethelburga, who was so beloved in her family that they called her Tata, the darling. Edwin sent messengers to ask Ethelburga's brother, Eadbald, who had succeeded his father as king, to give him his sister in marriage. But Eadbald said that he could not give his sister to a heathen. Edwin would not be refused. He sent messengers again, and said that if only he might have Ethelburga as his wife, he would allow her to worship in her own way, and would be willing to adopt her faith if, on hearing more about it, his wise men should decide that it was better than his own. So Ethelburga was sent to York with Bishop Paulinus as her chaplain. Edwin was true to his word; he treated Paulinus kindly, and after a while listened to his teaching, and when he had consulted his wise men, and they too were willing, he decided to be baptized.

Quickly a little wooden chapel was built on the spot where now stands the great minster of York, and within its walls Edwin and many others were taught the Christian faith. On Easter Eve, in the year 627, he was baptized. Many of his nobles as well as members of his family were baptized with him. Amongst them was a young girl, his great-niece, the Princess Hilda, then fourteen years old. We do not know anything about Hilda's life as a child nor for some years after her baptism. Her mother and her sister were also early converts to Christianity. In some way Hilda must have continued her Christian education, most probably she lived at a religious settlement in the north, and was busy in some sort of work for the Church. In those days all girls either married or entered a convent of some kind. Hilda, a member of a royal family, would certainly have been sought in marriage had it not been known that she had in some way given herself to a religious life. Many royal ladies were founders of convents. They received grants of land from their fathers or brothers and gathered round them those who wished to live in peace, away from all the fighting and disturbance of the world. Many royal ladies retired into convents after their husband's death, or sometimes even during their husband's lifetime. In the convents they could study, or do beautiful embroidery for the churches, care for the sick and aged, or teach the children. It was considered the holiest life that a woman could lead: those men, too, who wished to lead quiet lives and to spend their days in study rather than in fighting could only do so by retiring into a convent. If it had not been for the convents in early times there would have been no books, no learning, no art or industry. It was by the people who lived in the convents that the land was drained and cultivated, and that sheep and oxen were reared. France had become Christian earlier than England, so there were more famous convents there, and ladies belonging to the English royal families used to go over to the French convents to be educated, and often retired to them to end their days.

We are not told that Hilda was sent to a French convent to be educated, but her sister Hereswitha, who had married the King of East Anglia, went after his death to a French convent, and Hilda prepared to join her there. Hilda was by this time thirty-three. All that we know of her life since her baptism is what the old Northumbrian historian, Bede, tells us—that she lived very nobly among her family and fellow-citizens. Somehow her virtues and gifts attracted the notice of Aidan, the holy Bishop of Lindisfarne, who was working with zeal and devotion to win the wild people of the north for Christ. He seems to have been Hilda's friend and adviser, and he wanted her help in his work. When he heard that she was thinking of going to join her sister in France, he begged her to remain among her own people and to help them. Hilda yielded to his wishes, and she first settled down with a few companions on the river Wear. But soon afterwards she was called in the year 647, to be head of a convent in Hartlepool, which had been founded some years before, and was the first convent for women in that part of England.

Those were very anxious days. There had been Christian kings in Northumbria who had made it into a great and strong kingdom, and with the help of Aidan and other holy men had made the people Christian and brought peace into the land. But the Northumbrian kings were attacked by Penda, the last great heathen king in England, a fierce and mighty fighter, and it seemed at times as if he would utterly destroy the power of the

Christian kings. Hilda in her quiet convent must have waited anxiously for the news that came of the fighting between Oswy, the King of Northumbria, and Penda, who with his great army of fierce fighters seemed to rush like a torrent over the country. It was eight years after she had gone to Hartlepool, that Oswy with a much smaller army, utterly routed Penda's great host in a battle in which the fierce old heathen king was himself killed. Before the battle Oswy had sworn that if he gained the victory, he would give his infant daughter to God; and he now sent his little Ælflæd, not yet a year old, to his kinswoman Hilda to bring up in her convent. With his daughter, he gave also a rich gift of land, so that Hilda might be able to extend her work. The little Ælflæd was a great delight to Hilda, and grew up to be her dearest companion and fellow-worker.

Hilda had done much at Hartlepool. She had learnt all she could from wise men as to how to order a convent. Aidan and all the religious men who knew her used to visit her constantly. They were glad to teach her all they knew, and they loved her dearly because of her wisdom and her delight in the service of God.

In those days the work that women could do for the Church was highly esteemed, and the abbesses who ruled over the convents were very important people. They had to manage large estates as well as to order all the different kinds of work that were carried on in the convent. Many of them were very learned women; and we know of Hilda that she was always eager to learn, and knew well how to teach others what she had learnt. After she had spent some years at Hartlepool, she decided to found a new convent on some of the lands that had been granted her by King Oswy. She chose a beautiful spot on the top of a high cliff overlooking the sea, at the mouth of the river Esk. This spot was afterwards called Whitby, and by that name Hilda's famous abbey is best known. But though in later times a beautiful abbey church was built there, the ruins of which are still standing, all that Hilda could build was a rude little church made of the split trunks of trees, thatched with rushes. Round the church stood the huts in which Hilda and her nuns lived, with their kitchen and their dining-hall. Farther off, but still in the enclosure of the convent, were huts in which monks lived; for in those early days it often happened that men and women joined together to found one convent. The monks and the nuns lived apart, but Hilda ruled over them all alike. Some of the monks tilled the fields belonging to the convent: and there were barns and farm buildings, as well as rooms for writing and study. Over all these different men and women Hilda ruled firmly and wisely. They were all treated alike. There was no one in her convent who was rich and no one who was poor, for those who came there gave all their possessions into the common store. Hilda so ruled that peace and charity prevailed amongst them all. All who knew her called her Mother, because of her singular piety and grace, and the fame of her virtues spread far and wide. She loved learning and wished all to study, and made them give much time to the reading of the Bible. Her own wisdom and prudence were so well known that many people, and amongst them even kings and princes, came to her for advice in their difficulties. Amongst those who studied at Whitby many grew afterwards to be famous, and five of those who had lived under Hilda's rule became bishops of the Church. But, of all the dwellers at Whitby, the most famous was one who had begun life simply as one of the workers on the farm, the sweet singer Cædmon.

Photo: Frith & Co.
Whitby Abbey. This was the successor of St. Hilda's building.

In those days, at feasts, it was the custom for one after another to be asked for a song, and the harp was passed round the table, each taking it in turn and accompanying himself whilst he sang.

Cædmon thought that he could not sing, and when he saw that his turn was coming near, he used to get up and quietly leave the table and go home. One day he had left the feast in this way and gone to the stable where it was his duty that night to take care of the horses. Having done his work he settled himself to sleep, and in the night one stood by his side, and calling to him, said, "Cædmon, sing some song to me." He answered,

"I cannot sing, for that reason I left the feast and withdrew to this place, because I cannot sing." But he who stood by his side answered, "However, you shall sing." "What shall I sing?" asked Cædmon; and the answer came, "Sing the beginning of created beings." Then in his dream he sang in praise of God the Creator with words which he had never heard before. When he awoke, he remembered what he had sung, and added more verses to those which had come to him in his dream. He told the steward who was set over him of this gift of song that had been granted to him in his sleep, and the steward took him to the Abbess Hilda. She bade him in the presence of herself and of several learned men repeat the verses which he had made, and they all decided that it must be through the grace of God that this gift had come to him. They explained to him a passage from the Bible and bade him go away and turn it into verse. Next morning he came back and recited to them the excellent verses which he had made. Then Hilda bade him give up his work on the farm and come into the convent and become a monk, that he might devote himself to cultivating the gift of song which he had received. She directed some of the brethren to teach him the sacred history contained in the Bible, that he might turn it into song. After they had taught him, Cædmon would think over all that he had heard, turning it over in his mind as the cow chews the cud, till he brought it out again as harmonious verse, which he would sweetly repeat to his masters, who now in their turn became his hearers. He sang of the Creation and of the doings of the people of Israel and of the life and sufferings of the Lord Jesus Christ, and tried by his poems to lead men to love virtue and hate vice. Through his sweet singing great fame came to Hilda's convent, and after some years he died there in great peace and holiness.

We are not told whether Hilda was able as time went on to build a more stately church in place of the rough wooden one which she at first put up, but it seems most likely, considering the fame of her abbey, that she must have done so. She probably was friendly with Benedict Biscop, the Abbot of Wearmouth, which was also in the north of England. Benedict Biscop had made many journeys to France and Italy, and he first brought to England glass windows and beautiful vestments for his church, as well as skilled masons and glass workers from France, who taught their craft to the Northumbrians. We cannot doubt that Hilda with her energy and her wisdom got some of these men to come and teach her people also how to put up beautiful buildings; perhaps Benedict Biscop may have given her some of the treasures, vestments, pictures, or vessels for the church services which he had brought back with him. The fame and importance of the Abbey of Whitby is shown by the fact that it was chosen as the spot in which to hold a great Council of the Church in 664, when many bishops met with King Oswy to settle matters of great importance for the whole Church in England. Hilda had to care for the entertainment of this great gathering and to take part in their discussions. They had met to decide whether in certain matters the customs of the Church of Rome or the customs of the Church in Northumbria should be followed. Hilda was in favour of the customs of Northumbria, but when King Oswy decided that it would be better to do as the rest of the Church did, she was wise enough to give in to his decision, seeing that these were matters which concerned only the order and not the teaching of the Church.

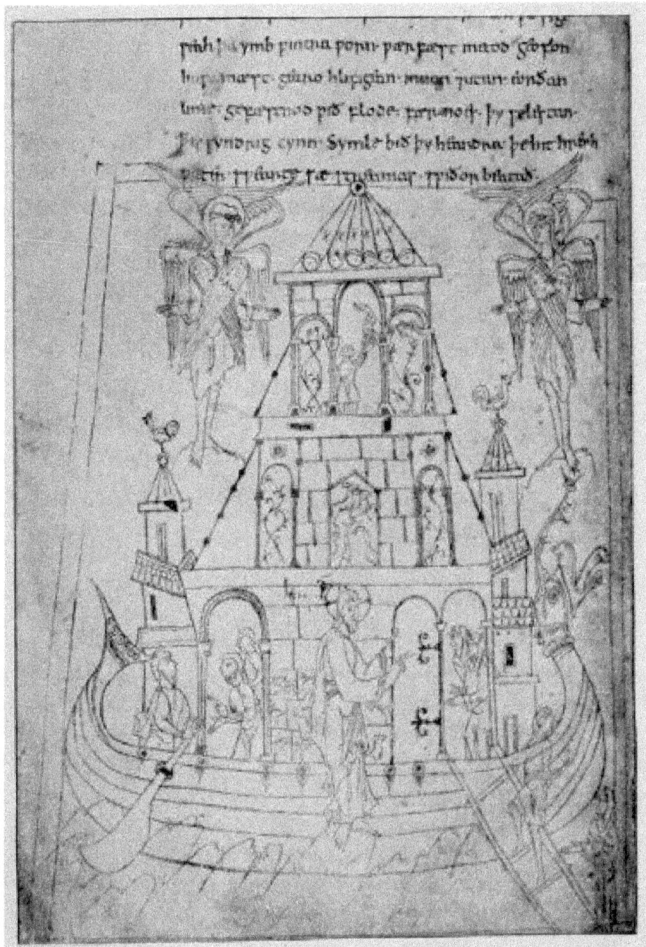

The Completion of the Ark. From the Cædmon MS.,
circa A.D. 1000, in the Bodleian Library, Oxford.

We know that Hilda founded at least one other convent herself, and several others were founded in different parts of England in imitation of the great Abbey of Whitby. For many years she ruled her convent with wisdom and diligence. At the end of her life she was called to bear the trial of a long illness. For six years she lay ill, but during all that time whenever possible, she would still teach those under her rule. She bade them serve God dutifully when they were in perfect health, and always return thanks to Him even when in trouble or suffering. How to do this she showed by her own example, for all through her long sickness she never failed to return thanks to God. When at last she felt death drawing near, she gathered all the inmates of her convent around her, and having bidden them to live in peace with one another and with all others, she joyfully welcomed death who came to take her from her sufferings to new life. She died in 680 at the age of sixty-six.

Ælflæd, the daughter of King Oswy, who as an infant had been confided to Hilda's care, succeeded her as abbess. Hilda was honoured as a saint by the Church after her death.

CHAPTER II

Joan, the fair maid of Kent

··· ✧ ···

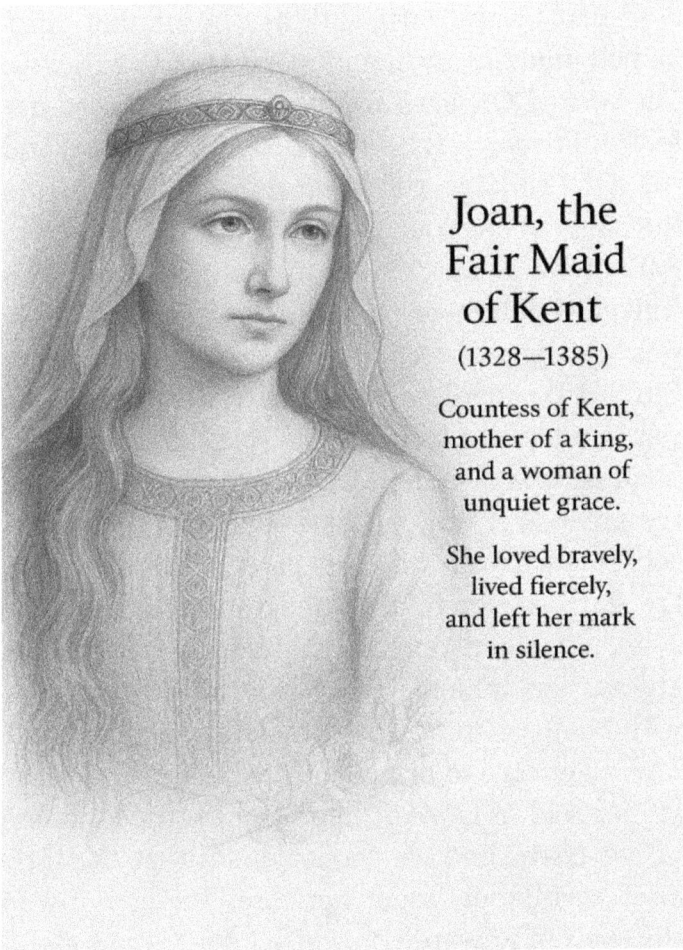

Joan, the Fair Maid of Kent
(1328—1385)

Countess of Kent, mother of a king, and a woman of unquiet grace.

She loved bravely, lived fiercely, and left her mark in silence.

On the 19th March 1329, a great English noble, Edmund, Earl of Kent, was beheaded outside the walls of Winchester. He was the youngest son of one of England's noblest kings, Edward I.; but he was a weak, vain man, and in the troublous days which followed Edward I.'s death he had been used first by one party and then by another, until he had made many enemies and kept few friends. The wicked Queen Isabella, who had allowed her foolish husband, Edward II., to be murdered, and ruled the country with her favourite, Mortimer, in the name of her young son, Edward III., hated the Earl of Kent. She vowed his ruin and had him convicted of treason. Men did not love Kent, but it was thought a terrible thing that the son of Edward I. should perish like a traitor. Though he was condemned to death, no one dared lift their hand against him, and from morning till evening the great Earl waited, till a condemned criminal consented to win his own pardon by cutting off the Earl's head. Kent's youngest child, the little Joan, was then only a year old, and two years afterwards Philippa, Queen of Edward III., moved with compassion for her desolate state, took her under her care to bring her up at her court. Many stories told of Queen Philippa show the kindness of her heart, and we cannot doubt that the little Joan was happy under her care. She grew up in the court of Edward III., which after his successful wars in France became one of the most magnificent in Europe. Life was a ceaseless round of festivities and gaieties. Rich booty was brought back from the French wars, and the English ladies copied the extravagant fashions of the French. We read of the feather beds with gorgeous hangings which were used, of the rich furs, of the velvet robes embroidered in silk and pearls, of the trailing dresses which lay in heaps upon the ground in front as well as behind. Joan grew up to be a very beautiful girl and to be very fond of fine clothes. She is said to have been full of charm and to have been clever and brilliant as well. The king's eldest son, Edward, afterwards known as the Black Prince, was two years younger than she, and growing up together, they seem to have learnt to love one another.

Tournament.

It was natural that Joan, who is described as the most beautiful and the most lovable of all the maidens of England, should have had many suitors. Her heart was won by Sir Thomas Holland, but whilst he was away at the wars, the Earl of Salisbury tried to win her as his wife. When Holland came back he petitioned the Pope to affirm his right to Joan's hand, and after both sides had been heard, judgment was given that Joan was the wife of Holland. She was then just twenty-one, and shortly afterwards, as both her brothers died, she became her father's heiress and Countess of Kent. Her husband was given various appointments in France, and Joan went there with him several times. She always surrounded herself with luxury of every kind and spent a great deal of money on dress. Holland died in 1360 leaving her still beautiful and charming, with three children. She was at once sought in marriage by many suitors, but she would listen to none of them. An old writer tells us that one day the Black Prince visited her and tried to persuade her to accept one of these suitors, who was a friend of his. She constantly refused, and at last answered, weeping, that she had given herself to the most noble knight under heaven, and that for love of him she would have no other husband as long as she lived, but that she knew that he could never be hers.

Then the Prince implored her to tell him who this most noble knight was, and when she would not speak, he went down on his knees saying that if she would not tell him, he would be her mortal enemy. At last he wrung from her the confession that it was he himself whom she meant, and when he heard this, he was filled with love for her, and vowed that he would never have any other wife so long as he lived. Edward was then thirty years of age, and had refused many princely offers of marriage. Perhaps he had never forgotten the beautiful cousin who had grown up with him, and now when she was free he rejoiced to make her his. It is said that Edward III. was very displeased when he heard that his son had made a marriage contract with Joan, but that Queen Philippa, who had always loved her tenderly, took their part. However this may be, we know that they were married by the Archbishop of Canterbury at Windsor, in the presence of the King, only ten months after the death of Joan's first husband. The marriage took place in October, and they went afterwards to the Prince's castle at Berkhamsted, where they spent Christmas.

In those days a great part of France was under the rule of the King of England, and the knights and nobles of the fair Duchy of Aquitaine which had belonged to the kings of England since the day when it had come to Henry II. through his wife Eleanor, asked Edward III. to send his son to rule over them. The Black Prince was famous for his courage and for the great victories he had won in battle against the King of France. Edward III. thought it only right that his son should have a distinguished position, and he appointed him Prince of Aquitaine. Then the Black Prince and Joan made great preparations for their departure, for they were determined to have a magnificent court in Aquitaine and to take with them many English knights and nobles. The English Parliament found it difficult to provide the large sums of money needed for the luxurious lives of Edward III. and his sons. It was hoped that Aquitaine would be able to provide for the needs of the Black Prince and his wife. But they spent so much before their departure in entertaining the King and court for Christmas at their castle, and in supplying themselves with clothes and furniture and all things needed for their journey, that they left England deeply in debt.

Early in the year 1363, they landed at La Rochelle and were received by a great company of knights and gentlemen who welcomed them with much joy. Four days were spent at La Rochelle in feastings and merriment, and then they set out on their journey to Bordeaux. At every town through which they passed, they were received by all the nobles of the neighbourhood, who crowded to do homage to the Prince.

Aquitaine was a rich and flourishing country, covered with vineyards, and carried on a vigorous wine trade with England. The Prince set up his court at Bordeaux, and it soon became the most brilliant court in Europe. Both the Prince and Princess were alike in being very extravagant and in loving fine clothes and merry-making. Those were the days of chivalry, when the knights were brave and courteous to one another, and loved jousts and tournaments in which they fought together in the presence of noble ladies, and the winner received the prize for his valour from the hand of a fair lady. But in their pursuit of pleasure, the princes and nobles forgot their duties as wise rulers. As long as they could win fame for themselves, and get enough money for their wars and their luxuries, they cared very little for the well-being of the people. In the Black Prince's court at Bordeaux, the pride and magnificence and neglect of the needs of the people which were the weakness of chivalry showed themselves most clearly.

The Black Prince was a noble host; he made every one around him happy. Eighty knights and four times as many squires feasted every day at his table. The princess never showed herself except surrounded by many ladies and fair maidens. The luxury of their dress, the strange new fashions in which their clothes were cut and their wonderful head-dresses embroidered with pearls shocked the people, who had been accustomed to simpler and severer manners. The princess seems never to have remembered that the money to pay for all these luxuries had to be wrung by taxation from the people. In other ways she ever showed herself warm-hearted and generous, and herself on one occasion pleaded with one of the nobles to diminish the ransom due to him from a prisoner taken in war.

Knight Receiving his Helmet from Lady.

The joyous life at Bordeaux was crowned by the birth of a son. Soon afterwards there began to be talk of war with Spain, and it was decided that the Black Prince should lead an expedition there. Great was the despair of the princess when she heard that he was to go. The old chronicler tells us that she lamented bitterly, saying, "Alas! what will happen to me if I shall lose the true flower of gentleness, the flower of magnanimity—him who in the world has no equal for courage? I have no heart, no blood, no veins, but every member fails me when I think of his departure." But when the prince heard her lamentations, he comforted her and said, "Lady, cease your lament and be not dismayed, for God is able to do all things." He took his leave of her very tenderly and said, lovingly, "Lady, we shall meet again in such case that we shall have joy both we and all our friends; for my heart tells me this." Then they embraced with many tears, and all the dames and damsels of the court wept also, some weeping for their lovers, some for their husbands.

Shortly before the prince's departure, Joan had given birth to a second son, Richard, called Richard of Bordeaux, from the place of his birth, who afterwards became King Richard II. The Black Prince was away in Spain for a year. He was victorious in the war and on his return he was magnificently welcomed at Bordeaux. A solemn procession of priests bearing crosses came out to meet him, followed by the princess with her elder son then three years old, surrounded by her ladies and her knights. They were full of joy at their meeting, and after tenderly embracing they walked hand in hand to their palace.

For the moment all seemed happy, but it soon appeared that the prince had come back tired and worn out. He had succeeded in Spain, but the cause for which he had fought was not a just one. The people of Aquitaine were discontented because of the heavy taxes they had to pay to keep up his luxurious court. It seemed to his enemies a good moment to attack him, and the King of France, anxious to win back some of the lands that he had lost, declared war against the English.

When the war began, the Black Prince was helpless with illness. He was so furious with the French that he had himself carried in a litter to attack them, and, for the first time, he showed himself cruel to the people he conquered. Everything seemed to go wrong. Their eldest son died, to the great grief of the prince and princess, and at last the prince was so ill that he had to give up the command of his army to his brother, John of Gaunt, Duke of Lancaster, and return to England. It was a sad coming home, very different from their joyous setting out for France. In England, too, things were going badly; the king was old, and the people were discontented because of the extravagance of the court and the nobles. The Black Prince and his wife retired to their castle at Berkhamsted. He was afflicted with a grievous malady and suffered terribly, but he interested himself in the affairs of the country and supported the Parliament, which was trying to remedy some of the abuses of the government. In order to do this, he moved up to London to the royal palace at Westminster. It was there that he died after four years of illness and suffering. He commended his wife and his little son Richard to the care of his father and brothers, and begged his followers that as they had served him, so they would serve his little son. The princess was broken-hearted at her husband's death and bewailed herself with bitter tears and lamentations. She was named guardian of her little son Richard, who was then ten years old; he was made Prince of Wales and declared heir to the throne, and only a year passed before, at his grandfather's death, he became King of England.

Those were anxious days in England. The country was worn out with the expenses of long wars and of an extravagant court. The people had suffered from a terrible pestilence called the Black Death. Everywhere there was want and scarcity, which led to bitter discontent. The boy king was surrounded by his uncles, ambitious men, who each wished to be the chief power in the country. His mother, the Princess Joan, does not seem to have had any ambition to take part in public affairs; we do not hear of her mixing herself up in any of the intrigues that went on round the little king; only once or twice she seems to have come forward to make peace. She is said to have been interested in the teaching of John Wiclif, a learned clergyman. Disgusted with the corruption of many of the clergy, he was trying to teach a purer faith, and he had translated the Bible into English so that even the unlearned might read it. But we hear so little about Joan that it is clear that she must have lived very quietly during these troubled days.

The discontent of the people at last led the peasants to rise in revolt in many different parts of the country, and to march on London in order to get redress for their wrongs. Princess Joan had been on a pilgrimage to Canterbury, where the Black Prince lay buried, when, on her way back, she fell in on crossing Blackheath with a crowd of the rebels. The rough men surrounded her, but the charm and beauty which she still possessed won their respect and the protection of their leaders. It is said that, after asking her for some kisses, they allowed her to pass on her way unharmed. She went to join her son in the Tower. Richard, then a boy of fifteen, was not frightened by the rebels, who swarmed round the Tower and asked that the king should come out and hear their grievances. He rode out with one or two followers and went to meet the rebels at Mile End, where he promised all that they asked him. But whilst he was away, another band of rebels broke into the Tower. They forced their way into the princess's room and treated her with rough familiarity and rudeness. They plunged daggers into her bed to see if anything was hidden there, and terrified her so much that she fainted. Then her ladies carried her away, and conveyed her in an open boat across the river to a house belonging to the king called the Wardrobe, and there Richard joined her. Meanwhile the rebels had seized and murdered the Archbishop, the chief minister of the king. In the end the rebels were put down after much bloodshed.

Richard II. seems to have had the charm and beauty of his mother, and as a boy at least, the courage of his father, but he did not grow up to be a wise king. He quarrelled with his powerful uncle, John of Gaunt, Duke of Lancaster, who was suspected of wishing to make himself king, and John, angry with his nephew, shut himself up in his castle at Pontefract. The Princess Joan was ill and had grown so stout that travelling was very difficult for her, but in spite of her sufferings she made several journeys to Pontefract to see John of Gaunt and at last succeeded in reconciling him with Richard. Richard treated her with great respect, and when he went away to make war in Scotland, he appointed five noble gentlemen to stay with her for her protection, wherever she chose to live. But she could not always persuade him to do as she wished. Her son by her first marriage, John Holland, had a quarrel with another gentleman and slew him treacherously. Richard to punish him seized his lands, and when Joan implored his pardon refused to listen to her. This so grieved her that she fell ill and died whilst Richard was still away in Scotland. In her will she asked to be buried near her first husband in the church at Stamford; and there on Richard's return her funeral took place. The quarrels between her son and his uncles which she had tried to heal grew worse after her death, till they ended in the deposition of Richard, and the choice of John of Gaunt's son, Henry, as king.

Joan was not in any way a great woman, but we feel that there must have been something uncommon about her beauty and her charm for the memory of it to have lasted as it did. It was some time after her death that the name of the Fair Maid of Kent was given her. She is an example of the great lady of those days, kindly, generous, loving brave men, trying to promote peace and kindliness, but extravagant and pleasure-seeking. No evil is told of her, and she seems to have loved both her husbands dearly and to have won their love in return.

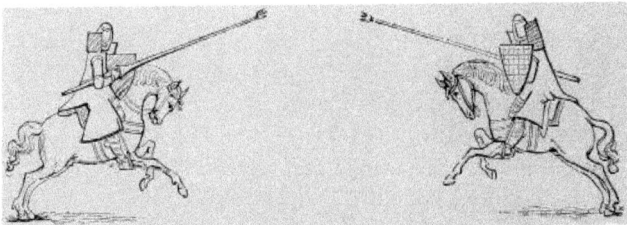

Knights Jousting.

CHAPTER III

Jeanne d'Arc, the maid of France

... ✦ ...

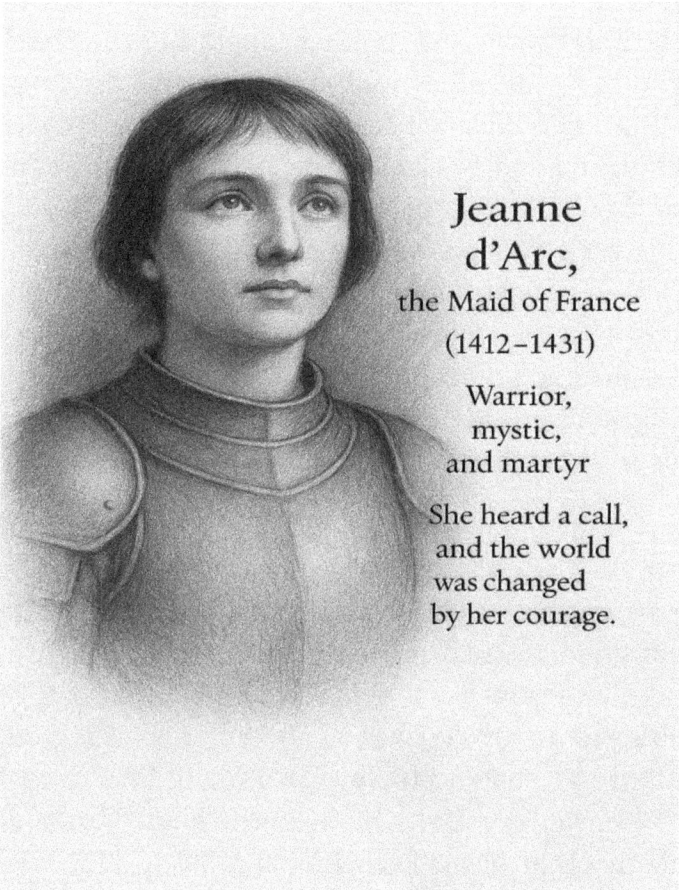

Jeanne d'Arc,
the Maid of France
(1412–1431)

Warrior,
mystic,
and martyr

She heard a call,
and the world
was changed
by her courage.

On January 6, probably in the year 1412, Jeanne d'Arc was born in Domremy, a little village in Lorraine, the great duchy which lies on the eastern frontier of France. Jeanne's father was a hard-working peasant. He owned horses and cattle and was one of the most respected inhabitants of his village. There were no village schools in those days and Jeanne never learnt to read and write. Her mother taught her the creed and her prayers, as well as sewing and the work about the house. Like other peasant girls she ploughed and worked in the fields and took care of the cattle. She played with the other children, and used to dance and weave garlands with them. Best of all she loved to go into the little church and pray, so that sometimes the other children laughed at her for her piety. She used to nurse the sick, and would even lie all night upon the hearth in order to give up her bed to some poor person.

France was at that time in a very troubled state. The whole land was divided into two parties, the Burgundians and the Armagnacs. The Burgundians had made friends with the English, who under Henry V. had conquered great part of France. Henry V. was dead, but his little son, Henry VI., had been crowned King of France, and his uncle, the Duke of Bedford, held Paris and many other towns in the north of France for him. The true King of France, Charles VII., had not been crowned yet, and many people still called him the Dauphin, the name by which the eldest son of the King of France used to be called. He was quite young, of a slow and lazy disposition, and had lost heart, and did not know how to meet the difficulties which surrounded him. News of the sad state of France must often have reached Domremy, brought by travellers of all kinds, pedlars, pilgrims, and wandering friars, who carried the news in those days as the newspapers do now.

When Jeanne was about thirteen, at noon one summer's day, she was in her father's garden, when she suddenly saw a strange light and heard a voice speaking to her. She was filled with fear and wondered what this could mean. But she believed that it was the voice of God that she heard, and after hearing it thrice, she knew it to be the voice of an angel. Twice or thrice a week she used to hear the voice. It told her to be good and to go often to church, and it also told her that she must go into France. Sometimes there were several voices, and she thought they were the voices of the Archangel Michael and of the Saints Margaret and Catherine. Sometimes she saw their visible shapes, Michael in armour, the Saints crowned with fair crowns. Their voices were beautiful, gentle, and sweet, and a delicate fragrance accompanied them. We cannot explain these visions. Jeanne herself believed that she saw and heard the Saints, and that they guided her in all she had to do. After she had seen them, she grew still more devout in her prayers, but though again and again the voices told her to go into France, she waited from three to four years wondering what this could mean, and speaking to no one of the voices. In 1428, they told her to go to the governor of the neighbouring town, Vaucouleurs, and ask him for an armed escort into France, that she might save the town of Orleans, which was besieged by the English. She answered, "I am a poor girl, who cannot ride or be a leader in war." But at last the day came when she felt that she could not resist the voices any more. She did not tell her father and mother, but she asked permission to visit a married cousin who lived near Vaucouleurs. Then she persuaded her cousin's husband to take her to see the governor. The governor was a blunt, rough soldier, not at all likely to believe in Jeanne's mission. He could not be expected to think that an ignorant girl of sixteen could save France, and he seems only to have laughed at her. She went home not discouraged but quite clear in her mind that next year she would save the Dauphin, and take him to be crowned at Rheims, the city where the French kings had always been crowned.

Jeanne in Church.

In 1429 once more she went to Vaucouleurs. It was long before she could get the governor to listen, but her determination never wavered. She said, "I must be with the king by mid-lent if I wear my legs down to the knees." We do not know what at last prevailed upon the governor to let her go, but she found two men who believed in her mission who undertook to lead her to the king, and with them and their two servants she was allowed to start. By the advice of one of these friends, she decided to travel in a man's dress. She wore a tunic, with breeches and boots, and a page's cap. The people of Vaucouleurs gave her a horse. Her friends gathered to see her off, begging her not to go, and urging the dangers of the journey. But she answered, "The way is made clear before me. I have my Lord who makes the path smooth to the gentle Dauphin, for to do this deed I was born."

Jeanne hears the Voice.

Jeanne met with no difficulties on her journey right across France to Chinon, where the king was. At first he would not see her, but at last she was brought into his presence, where he sat surrounded by fifty knights in a hall blazing with fifty torches. No one told her which was the king, but she knew neither fear nor doubt. One who was there says that she came forward with great humility and simplicity, and spoke to the king: "Most noble Lord Dauphin, I come from God to help you and your realm." The king drew her apart and spoke to her for a long time. She told him that she would drive away the English from before Orleans, and that she would lead him to be crowned, and she told him other things which were kept secret between him and her; what they were she would never tell.

The king seemed to those who were watching to rejoice at what he heard, but he was always slow to move. He had to wait and consult many people and test the Maid in many ways to find out whether he might trust her, before he would let her do as she wished. In vain Jeanne prayed and wept, longing to be allowed to bring help to the people of Orleans. She was taken to the city of Poitiers and questioned by learned men. She was so bothered by their many questions that when one asked, "Do you believe in God?" she answered, "More firmly than you do." It was six weeks before it was decided that she might be trusted, and allowed to go to Orleans. Then a suit of steel armour was made for her. She wished to wear a special sword which she said that her voices had told her would be found behind the altar at a little church near Tours. It was found as she had said, covered with rust, which however came off easily when they began to clean it. The people of Tours gave her two splendid sheaths, one of red velvet and one of cloth of gold for the sword. In her hand she carried her standard, which was white, with angels painted on it and the motto "Jesus Maria." She never used her sword and never killed any one herself. Several men were chosen as her attendants and her two brothers joined her.

Jeanne Rides to Chinon.

When Jeanne was with the army, twice every day she gathered the priests who were there round her banner, and they prayed and sang hymns; men learnt to behave better for her presence. As she neared Orleans, Dunois one of the chief men in the French army, came out to meet her, and said that he was right glad of her coming. With him she made her way into Orleans past the English army. She entered the city by night lest the crowd should be too great; but many bearing torches came to meet her, and men, women, and children pressed lovingly around her. Her business now was to attack the forts which the English had built outside the town. But before she would allow this to be done, she insisted that the English should thrice be summoned to depart in peace. In her clear young voice (she was only seventeen) she cried to them across the river, and they shouted back insulting words saying they would burn her if they caught her. But just as Jeanne's coming had filled the French soldiers with new hope and courage, so it had terrified the English. They did not dare attack that slim figure in shining armour. At last the French from the other side began to attack the English forts. Jeanne, worn out, was resting on her bed, she did not know that the fighting had begun. But suddenly she woke with a cry saying that she must go against the English. Quickly her armour was buckled on, she sprang on her horse and was off. On the next five days there was fighting with the English, except on Ascension day, when Jeanne would not allow any one to go out. On the last day, the chief of the English forts was attacked and Jeanne led the attack. At noon as she mounted the first scaling ladder set against the wall, an arrow struck her shoulder, piercing her armour. She shrank and wept, but she barely paused to have her wound stanched, and went back to the front. When the sun was sinking and men doubted whether the fort could be taken, her voice was heard crying, "Doubt not, the place is ours." Her faithful followers rallied round her, and one seized her standard and dashed forwards. "Watch," Jeanne said, "till the tail of my standard touches the wall." When it did she said, "Then enter: all is yours." The last terrible assault carried all before it, and the fort was won. When Jeanne saw close at hand the terrors of war, she knelt weeping and praying for the souls of her enemies. Her first act was to go to the church and give thanks, after that she had her wound dressed.

A few days after this glorious victory, Jeanne went with Dunois to visit the Dauphin. Her good sense, which was one of the causes of her wonderful success, made her wish to press on to Rheims; besides her voices had told her that she would only have one year in which to do her work, and she was eager to get on. But the Dauphin hesitated and listened to other advice. "Noble Dauphin," Jeanne pleaded, "hold not such long and wordy councils, but come at once to Rheims and be worthily crowned." She could not persuade him to make haste, and the next month she spent in taking other places from the English. A young noble saw her at that time and wrote to his mother: "To see her and hear her speak, she seems a thing wholly divine."

At last her persistence was rewarded, and the Dauphin agreed to march to Rheims. The towns on their way yielded to him, or rather to Jeanne; it was she who ever filled her friends with courage and her foes with fear. Rheims opened its gates to them, and preparations were at once made for the coronation. When Charles was crowned in the great cathedral, the Maid stood next him with her standard in her hand, and when all was over she knelt, embracing his knees and weeping for joy, saying, "Gentle King, now is accomplished the will of God, who decreed that I should raise the siege of Orleans and bring you to this city of Rheims to receive your solemn sacring, thereby showing that you are the true king, and that France should be yours." In less than three months she had accomplished what she had set out from her village to do.

Jeanne is Wounded by the Arrow.

Jeanne had hoped that the day after the coronation, the king would set out for Paris, which was in the hands of his enemies. But again there were delays; Charles consented to make a truce of fifteen days with his enemies. Jeanne's good sense showed her what a mistake this was. Weary of the struggle, she longed that it might be God's pleasure for her to lay down her arms and return to keep her father and mother's sheep. But she would not leave her task. It was nearly six weeks before she was allowed to go against Paris, and she was so badly supported, that in spite of her great courage the attack failed. Once she stood all day in the ditch under the wall in the heat of the fire calling on the enemy to yield, till she was shot in the leg. Then when her men carried her under cover, though she could not move for her wound, she kept on crying out to them to charge, and telling them that the place was theirs if they would. But it was of no avail. Three days after the king decided to retreat and go back to the Loire. During most of the following winter there was little fighting, but in the spring once more Jeanne began to advance on Paris. It was then, one day in Easter week, that her voices told her that she would be captured before Midsummer day, adding that she must take all things well for God would help her. So they warned her every day, but never told her the hour of her captivity. Yet with this terrible fate before her, she rode on; she knew no turning back. A few weeks afterwards she was at Compiegne and led her men out against the enemy. They were surprised by an unexpected attack as they rode. Thrice Jeanne charged, and drove back the enemy, but more and more soldiers came up; most of Jeanne's men fled, only a few faithful ones stayed with her. The enemy surrounded them and Jeanne was forced from her horse, and carried off. Great was the joy of the English and their French friend, the Duke of Burgundy, when they heard that Jeanne was a prisoner. She was in the hands of a French noble of the English party, and was treated as a prisoner of war, but her enemies planned to sell her to the English, who had always said they would burn her if they could get her. Meanwhile she was kept in the castle of Beaurevoir, and kindly treated by the ladies of the castle. They wished her to lay aside her man's dress, but she refused, saying that she had not yet had leave from God. She did not feel that her mission was ended. She was much distressed by the stories that she heard of the sufferings of the people of Compiegne, the town which she was trying to relieve when she was taken prisoner. She longed to go and help them. She knew, too, that she was to be sold to the English and she dreaded falling into their hands. So one night she tried to escape by leaping from the tower, a height of sixty feet. She was found lying insensible in the ditch, but with no bones broken. She said afterwards that her voices had bidden her not to leap and had told her that Compiegne would be saved. Now the voices comforted her, bidding her beg God's pardon for having leaped.

The Coronation of Charles VII.

Jeanne soon recovered from her injuries, and Compiegne was indeed relieved, but the Maid was sold to the English after she had been some four months a prisoner. She was carried to several different places, and at last to Rouen, where she was imprisoned in the castle with rough, rude men to guard her. No woman was allowed to come near her; she was kept in chains, and night and day had to endure the company of the soldiers. It was because she still hoped that some way of escape might be shown her, that she would not give her promise not to try to escape. Had she done so, she might have been more kindly treated; but her great courage made her ready to bear anything, rather than give up the chance of going back to her task.

Jeanne was to be tried by the Church, because the plan of the English was to treat her as a witch inspired by devils. A French bishop, belonging to the English party, was the chief of her judges, and with him sat forty-three learned lawyers and clergy to judge the peasant girl of eighteen, before whom the English army had shrunk in terror. The Maid had already been nine months a prisoner when she was brought to trial. She appeared dressed in a black suit like a page, strong in her confidence in the guidance of God, and trusting in her voices to tell her what to answer. The judges could not make her swear to answer truthfully all their questions. She swore to speak the truth on certain subjects, but on others, chiefly on her private communications to the king, she said she would say nothing. First, for six long days she was questioned in the public court, the ignorant peasant girl alone amongst her enemies. She never faltered, her answers came quick and ready, though often her judges wearied her by going again and again over the same points. When they asked if she often heard her voices, she said that there was no day when she did not hear them, and she had great need of them. She described once how the voice had awakened her, and she had risen and sat on her bed with folded hands to listen and to give thanks for its coming. Always she showed that all that she had done had been done at the bidding of God. "I would rather have been torn in pieces by four horses than have come into France without God's command," she said. She stated confidently her belief that her king would gain the kingdom of France, adding that it was this revelation that comforted her every day. She never complained, and said that since it had pleased God to allow it, she believed that it was best that she should have been taken. She said that her voices encouraged her to bear her martyrdom patiently, for she would at last come to the heavenly kingdom. When she was asked what she meant by speaking of her martyrdom, she answered that she meant the pains she suffered in prison, and that she thought it probable she would have pains still greater to bear.

For six days she was publicly examined in court, and later, on nine other days, she was secretly examined in prison. During all this time, in spite of her constant entreaties, she was not allowed to hear Mass. On her way to the court she passed in front of a little chapel and she used to kneel to pray at the entrance till even this was forbidden. When at last her examination was finished, a long statement was drawn up in which Jeanne was declared to be a witch and a heretic and accused of many evil deeds. These accusations were sent to many learned men for their opinion, and all declared that Jeanne's voices were either inventions or the work of the devil, and that she was a liar. Meanwhile her judges visited her in prison and exhorted her to submit and own that she had been deceived. It was nearly two months since the beginning of her trial. Long sermons were preached at her; she was confused by many questions, difficult for an ignorant girl to answer, and told that it was her duty to submit to the Church. Again and again she answered simply, "I submit to God my Creator." She was ill and worn out with suffering and anxiety. But as she lay upon her bed in prison, she still answered bravely through her weariness, "Come what may, I will do or say no other thing." For a week she lay in her chains, the rude soldiers always with her. Then again others visited her urging her to confess, but she said, "If I saw the fire lit, if I were in the flames, I would say no other thing."

To the last she had hoped that deliverance would come somehow, but now it seemed to her that she was altogether deserted. On the 24th of May she was taken out to the stake in the market-place at Rouen, amongst a shouting crowd of hostile people. There a statement of the accusations against her was read out, and she said that she was willing to do as the Church ordered, and that since the doctors of the Church had decided that her visions and voices were not to be believed in, she would not defend them. She was bidden to sign a paper to this effect, and told that if she did so her life would be spared. We do not know what the paper was that at last Jeanne in her fear and weariness, consented to sign with her mark, and we do not know whether she understood what she signed. But a few days afterwards she said, "My voices have told me since that I greatly sinned in that deed, in confessing that I had done ill. What I said, I said in fear of fire."

Jeanne was now handed over to the Church to spend her life in prison. She cried, "Here, some of you church folk, take me to your prisons, and out of the hands of the English." But her judge sent her back to the same horrible prison with the English soldiers. A woman's dress was brought her and she was bidden to wear it. For three days she lay in prison with her legs in irons and chained to a wooden beam. We do not know exactly what happened, but on the third day, it was announced that Jeanne was again wearing the man's dress which she had sworn to her judges that she would not wear again. News was at once taken to the judges that she had relapsed, and they hurried to ask her the reason. She pleaded that it was more convenient to wear men's dress among men, and said, "I would rather die than remain in irons. If you will release me, and let me go to Mass and lie in gentle prison, I will be good and do what the Church desires." But there was no pity for her. It was decided that she must be given up by the Church to the English to be burnt. It is said that Jeanne cried piteously and tore her hair when she was told her fate. If so, she soon regained her courage. Her last desire was granted her; she was allowed to receive the sacrament. Then she was led out to the market-place, weeping as she went, so that she so moved the hearts of those who were with her and they also wept. She had to wait in the sight of a great crowd whilst a sermon was preached at her. When it was over, she humbly asked forgiveness of all and said that she forgave the evil that had been done her. Some who watched were moved to tears, but others were impatient to get away to dinner; so the bailiff said "Away with her." Then Jeanne was led to the scaffold piled with faggots. She climbed it bravely, but asked for a cross to hold as she burnt. There was none for her, till an English soldier broke his staff and made a little cross and gave it her. She kissed it and cried to her Saviour for help. To the last she affirmed that she was sure that her voices had come from God and had not deceived her. As she was being chained to the stake, she said, "Ah, Rouen, I fear greatly that thou mayst have to suffer for my death." Then as the smoke rose round her, she cried upon the Saints who had befriended her, and with a last strong cry "Jesus," her head sank and she was free from her pain.

The burning of Jeanne.

The story of Jeanne, the Maid of France, seems too wonderful to be true; but all that we know about her is taken from the words of those who knew and saw her, and from her own words at her trial, recorded not by her friends but by her enemies. It is by her own words that we know her best, and they show us her pure nature, her marvellous courage, her perfect devotion to the task given to her. We cannot explain what her voices were, but we know that she believed she heard them, and that somehow this simple peasant maid was taught how to save her king. She accomplished her task. It was she who gave

73

the French courage in their hour of despair, and in the end the English were driven out of the land and Charles VII. became king of the whole of France.

CHAPTER IV

Lady Margaret Beaufort

... ✧ ...

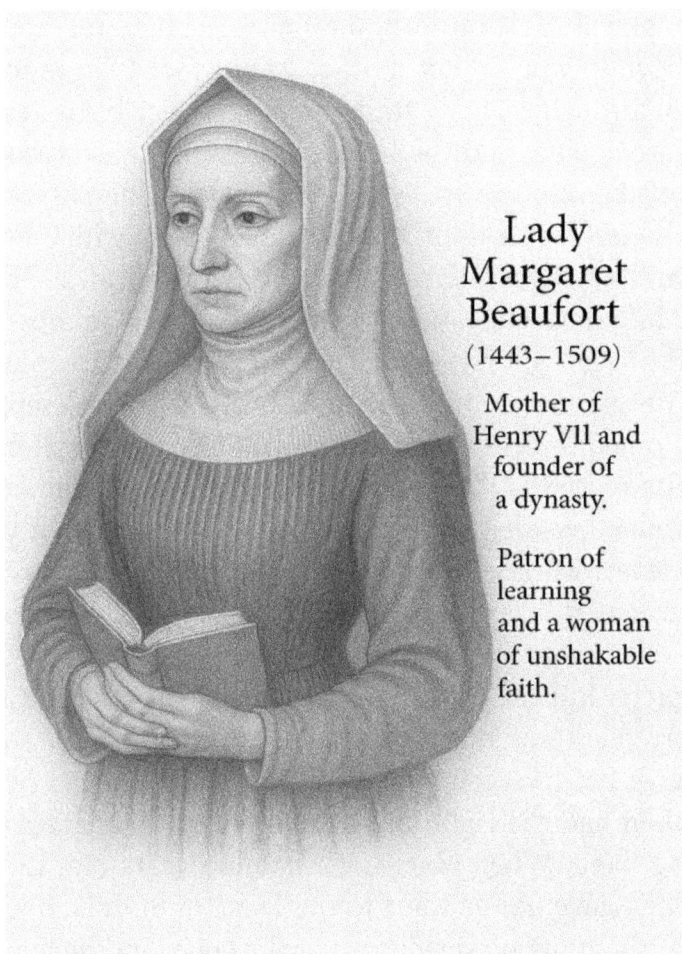

Lady
Margaret
Beaufort
(1443–1509)

Mother of
Henry VII and
founder of
a dynasty.

Patron of
learning
and a woman
of unshakable
faith.

It was in the beginning of the troubled times of the Wars of the Roses that Margaret Beaufort was born. Her father, the Duke of Somerset, was one of the great nobles on the Lancastrian side. He was the grandson of John of Gaunt, son of Edward III., and Duke of Lancaster, who had married a rich and noble heiress. Margaret was born in 1441 in her mother's manor of Bletsoe in Bedfordshire. Only three years after her birth her father died, and the little girl, his only child, was left heiress to vast estates and riches. She passed the early years of her life at Bletsoe with her mother. Great care seems to have been given to Margaret's education. It was not common in those days for girls even to be taught to write, but Margaret was bred in studious habits. She knew French perfectly, and also some Latin, but in later life regretted that she had not been able to gain a fuller knowledge of that language. She was very clever with her needle and is known to have executed beautiful embroidery. Above all she was well taught in religion and trained in habits of piety. But the condition of a great heiress was far from agreeable in those days. It was the custom to give her to some great noble as his ward, and he then had the right to arrange for her marriage as he liked. When Margaret was nine years old, the king gave her as ward to the Duke of Suffolk, one of the most powerful men of the time, and he had her brought to court, and wished to marry her to his son. But the king, Henry VI., wanted her to marry his half-brother, Edmund Tudor, Earl of Richmond. Margaret was puzzled by these different proposals, and asked the advice of an old lady whom she dearly loved. The old lady bade her ask St. Nicholas, a saint who was thought to care specially for young girls, to help her in this difficult matter. Margaret prayed often to St. Nicholas, and one night, whether she was awake or asleep she did not know, St. Nicholas in the dress of a bishop appeared before her and told her to take Edmund Tudor as her husband. This dream seems to have decided the choice of her mother, and as shortly afterwards the Duke of Suffolk fell into disgrace, it came about that Margaret was allowed to marry Edmund Tudor, when she was not quite fifteen years old. After her marriage she went with her husband to live at his castle of Pembroke in Wales, his native country. Only a year afterwards he died, and a few weeks after his death her son Henry was born. At the age of sixteen, only a child herself, she was left a widow, with a child to take care of.

The baby was small and weakly and to it Margaret gave all her care. It was an anxious time for the members of the Lancastrian family. Their rivals the Yorkists were beginning to rise into power, and the little Henry, both on account of his great possessions and because through his descent from John of Gaunt he was so nearly related to King Henry VI., was not likely to find them friendly to him and his mother. Margaret was glad to stay in quiet seclusion at Pembroke Castle under the protection of Jasper Tudor, her husband's brother, now owner of the castle.

Even had he wished, Henry VI. could not have befriended her. He was powerless, sometimes in the hands of those who called themselves his friends, sometimes flying before his enemies, whilst the country was distracted with the struggles of the Yorkists and the Lancastrians. Margaret thought it best to seek a protector for herself and her son by marrying Lord Henry Stafford. When Henry VI. was in power she and her son were able to visit the court, but at other times she was only safe in her castle in Wales. At last Edward of York became king as Edward IV. and Henry VI. was cast as a prisoner into the Tower. Edward IV. seized the lands belonging to the little Henry, and his mother feared lest even his life might not be safe, so she was willing that he should escape to France under the care of his uncle Jasper.

Henry was then fourteen. Margaret had watched anxiously over his delicate childhood, moving him about to different places in Wales for the good of his health. He was an intelligent boy, and once when his uncle Jasper had taken him to court to see Henry VI., the king is reported to have said, when he looked at him, "Surely this is he to whom both we and our adversaries shall hereafter give place." His tutor said that he had never seen a boy of so much quickness in learning. But now the poor boy had to leave his mother and his country. The wind drove him and Jasper to land on the coast of Brittany, and when the Duke of Brittany heard of their arrival, he ordered them to be brought to his castle at Vannes. There he kept Henry as a sort of prisoner, but refused to give him up to Edward IV., and though not allowed to leave Vannes, he was at least safe.

Edward IV. From an original painting belonging to the Society of Antiquaries.

For fourteen years Henry was obliged to remain in Brittany, separated from his mother.

The Yorkist king, Edward IV., was on the throne, and Margaret, separated from her son, lived as quietly as possible on her estates in the country, anxious to save what she could of her money and her lands for Henry. She seems to have stayed in different parts of the country. Wherever she lived, she devoted herself to the care of the poor and the good of the Church. Staying at one of her houses in Devonshire, she found that the priest's house was at some distance from the church so that he had some way to walk to and fro. She therefore presented to the church for ever her own manor-house, with the land around it, for the priest's use, as it was close to the church. She lived chiefly at Collyweston in Northamptonshire, where she built herself a fine house. She was deeply religious, and during these long years she spent much of her time in prayer. She used to get up at five o'clock and spend the hours till ten, which was in those days the hour for dinner, in meditation and prayer. The rest of the day she spent partly in ministering to the wants of the poor and sick, partly in study. Books in those days, just before the introduction of printing, were scarce and precious. Margaret busied herself with translating into English some books of devotion from the French. Amongst other things she was the first to translate into English part of that famous book, "The Imitation," by Thomas à

Kempis, which has helped and comforted so many people. We know little of her second husband, and do not know how much he was with her. He died after they had been married twenty-two years, and in his will he spoke of Margaret with warm love and trust. Shortly after his death, Margaret married for a third time, Lord Stanley, himself a widower with a large family, and one of the most powerful nobles at the court of Edward IV. In those days great people married more from policy than from love. Margaret probably felt that, now that it seemed as if the power of the Yorkists was established, it would be well for her to gain the protection of a powerful noble at court, who might in time help to make it possible for her son to return to England. She now left her quiet life and came to live in a great house in London belonging to her husband. Very shortly afterwards everything was changed by the unexpected death of Edward IV. When his brother, the Duke of Gloucester, made himself king as Richard III., and caused his little nephews to be murdered in the Tower, there was such discontent in England that it seemed to the friends of the house of Lancaster a good opportunity to destroy the Yorkist power.

Richard III. From an original painting belonging to the Society of Antiquaries.

Margaret's son Henry, as the descendant of John of Gaunt, was the chief representative of the house of Lancaster. A plan was made to make him king and marry him to Elizabeth, the beautiful young daughter of Edward IV. The Duke of Buckingham, one of the chief nobles of the time and till now a friend and supporter of Richard III., was one of the chief movers in this plot. Margaret was travelling one day on the road between Bridgnorth and Worcester, on her way to visit a special shrine at Worcester, when she chanced to meet the Duke of Buckingham, journeying from Tewkesbury. He told her of the proposed plot, and she was naturally eager to help in anything which might bring back her son to her. Reginald Bray, a discreet man, who was in Margaret's service and helped in looking after her estates, was employed in communicating with Henry. The young prince found many friends, and a fleet was got together to bring him to England. But after he had started, a mighty storm arose, scattered his ships, and drove him back to the coast of France with such fury that he narrowly escaped with his life. For the moment all seemed lost. Richard III.'s suspicions were thoroughly aroused. He knew that Margaret had been communicating with her son, and he was very angry with her. But he did not dare to anger her powerful husband, Lord Stanley, by treating her too severely. He bade Stanley keep her safely in some secret place at home, without any servant or company, so that she might have no means of communicating with her son. Stanley himself was really in Henry's favour, and Richard beginning to suspect him seized his eldest son and kept him as a hostage for his father.

Henry VII. From an original picture in the National Portrait Gallery.

Somehow communications with Henry still went on, and in 1485 he landed in Wales, and all men flocked to join him. Stanley, who pretended to keep true to Richard to the last, deserted him just before the battle of Bosworth, where Richard was utterly defeated and killed. His crown was found hanging in a bush by Reginald Bray and brought to Stanley, who placed it on the head of Henry crying, "Long live King Henry VII." It seems likely that Henry first met his mother at Leicester after the battle. She had parted from him fifteen years before, when he was a boy of fourteen, she met him again as King of England. The right that Henry had to the throne came to him through his mother. She might have claimed to be queen herself, but she never thought of doing this, nor did she try to take any part in public affairs. Of course all her lands were restored to her, and she was called at court "the full noble Princess Margaret, Countess of Richmond, Mother of our Sovereign Lord the King." She now for the most part lived at her manor of Woking in Surrey, coming to court only on important occasions. Henry married Elizabeth, the tall golden-haired daughter of Edward IV., a few months after he became king, and Margaret seems to have been with her on all important occasions. Perhaps she may have domineered over her a little too much, for the Spanish envoy reported to his court that Elizabeth "was a very noble woman and much beloved, but that she was kept in subjection by her mother-in-law, the Countess of Richmond." At any rate, Margaret was by her side on all great occasions. Together they watched from behind a lattice the coronation of Henry in Westminster Abbey, and the banquet afterwards in Westminster Hall. Together they went in state in a barge to Greenwich to see a water fête arranged by the Lord Mayor in honour of the king's coronation, where, among other shows, they watched a dragon which was carried along in a barge and spouted fire into the Thames.

Elizabeth of York, Queen of Henry VII. From an original picture in the National Portrait Gallery.

Henry VII. always treated his mother with great consideration. Margaret seems to have been an authority on matters of etiquette, for before the birth of his first child, Henry asked her to draw up a set of rules about the ceremonies to be observed on the occasion. In these rules it is stated that there were to be two cradles of tree, meaning of wood, one large for state occasions, to be adorned with paintings and furnished with cloth of gold and ermine fur and crimson velvet. At its christening, the child was to carry a little taper in its hand, and 200 torches were to be borne before it to the altar. After the baptism, the torches and the little taper were to be lit and the child was to present the taper at the altar. It looks as if the love for grand ceremonies which distinguished the Tudors had been started by Margaret. Her own household was beautifully ordered. She had drawn up a set of rules for the guidance of all the servants and the ladies and gentlemen, who made up her household, and these rules were read aloud four times a year that all might know and observe them. She visited in turn all her different estates, spending some time at each so that she might see that each was well ordered, and hear the complaints of all those who had any grievances. She herself would constantly speak loving words of encouragement to her servants, bidding them all to do well and to live in peace with one another. She employed a band of minstrels of her own, who would sometimes wander round the country and perform before the king and the court. As was the custom in those days, many young gentlemen were educated in her household. Her care of the sick and suffering never failed. She would minister to them with her own hands, and twelve poor folk to whom she gave food and raiment lodged constantly in her house.

Neither did Margaret forget her interest in study. We are told by Bishop Fisher, who knew her well, that she was of singular wisdom far surpassing the common rate of women. She collected a great number of books both English and French, and she was a warm friend to William Caxton, who first introduced printing into England, and who dedicated a book to her which he said had been translated from the French at her request. After Caxton's death in 1496, his assistant, Wynkyn de Worde, became the chief printer in London: he was much favoured by Margaret, and allowed to call himself, "Printer unto the most excellent princess, my lady the king's mother." He published books for Margaret, and amongst others one which she had herself translated from the French.

Margaret had always been a deeply religious woman, but with growing years she gave ever more time to her religious observances. Many hours were spent in prayer and in services in her chapel. She observed strictly all the fasts ordained by the Church, which were very severe in those days, and she wore on certain days in each week a hair shirt, or a hair girdle, next her skin in order to mortify her flesh. In 1497 Margaret appointed a learned Cambridge scholar, John Fisher, whom she had noticed with favour at court, where he had come on business connected with his university, to be her confessor. Fisher gained great influence over her, and he used it for the good of his university, which was then by no means in a prosperous condition. Margaret was always generous with her money; Fisher says of her that she hated avarice and covetousness, and she was glad to use her wealth to promote the cause of learning. Under Fisher's guidance she founded professorships at Cambridge and Oxford, which are still called after her. The college where Fisher had himself studied, called God's House, was very poor, and Margaret refounded it under the name of Christ's College, and herself made the statutes under which it was to be governed. She took great interest in it, and kept some rooms in it for herself, where she might stay when she came to Cambridge. Once when she was staying there, before the building of the College was finished, she was looking out of the window when she saw the dean beating a scholar who had misbehaved. She did not interfere to stop the punishment, but only called out in Latin, "Lente, Lente" (gently, gently), wishing that the beating might be less severe. It was in Cambridge that the famous scholar Erasmus met her on one of his visits to

England, when she was an old lady, and admired her good memory and her ready wit.

Before the buildings of Christ's College were finished, Fisher won Margaret's interest in the foundation of another college, St. John's. At that time, the time which is known as the Renaissance, because art and learning seemed to be born again, men were eager to improve the teaching at the universities, and to make it possible for all who wished to gain knowledge. Fisher was friends with Erasmus and other learned men, and Margaret was willing to help with her money his plans for the advancement of learning, just as she had helped Caxton and Wynkyn de Worde in printing and publishing books. But though, for those days, she was a learned woman herself, she does not seem to have thought that other women should be helped to study, and it was only the learning of men that she aided by her gifts.

Photo: A. E. Walsham.
Christ's College, Cambridge.

Henry VII. was interested in his mother's plans and himself visited Cambridge to see her college. He also thought highly of Fisher, and named him Bishop of Rochester. There seems to have been a deep affection between Henry and his mother. Once in writing to her, towards the end of his life, he says that he "is bounden to her for the great and singular motherly love and affection" she has always had for him. In writing to the king, Margaret called him "My own sweet and most dear king and all my worldly joy," and often addressed him as "my dear heart." She had the sorrow of seeing him die before her, but she did not live many months after him. She suffered greatly from rheumatic pains in what Bishop Fisher calls "her merciful and loving hands," so that her ladies and servants wept to see her agony. She died at Westminster and was buried in Henry VII.'s chapel in Westminster Abbey, where a black marble tomb commemorates her memory. Bishop Fisher preached her funeral sermon, and said in it "all England for her death had cause of weeping; the poor creatures that were wont to receive her alms, to whom she was always piteous and merciful, the students of both universities to whom she was a mother, all the learned men of England to whom she was a very patroness, all the good religious men and women, whom she so often was wont to visit and comfort." Margaret's plans for the foundation of St. John's College were not finished at her death, and Wolsey, the favourite of her grandson Henry VIII., tried to get her lands for other purposes. Fisher's efforts succeeded in keeping a great deal for St. John's, though not so much as Margaret had meant to give. She left all her jewels, books, vestments, plate, and altar cloths to her two colleges. She had been specially fond of fine goldsmith's work, and many beautiful things had been made for her, adorned with her own emblem, a daisy, or with the rose and the portcullis, which through her descent from the Lancaster and Beaufort families became the Tudor emblems. Besides her colleges, she founded several almshouses, and a school at Wimborne, where her parents were buried. She used her great possessions as a trust which she held for the good of the country, and for herself sought no luxury or display, being, as Bishop Fisher says in his sermon, "temperate in meats and drinks, eschewing banquets and keeping fast days."

Tudor Rose (white and red). From the gates of the Chapel of Henry VII.

CHAPTER V

Rachel, Lady Russell

··· ✦ ···

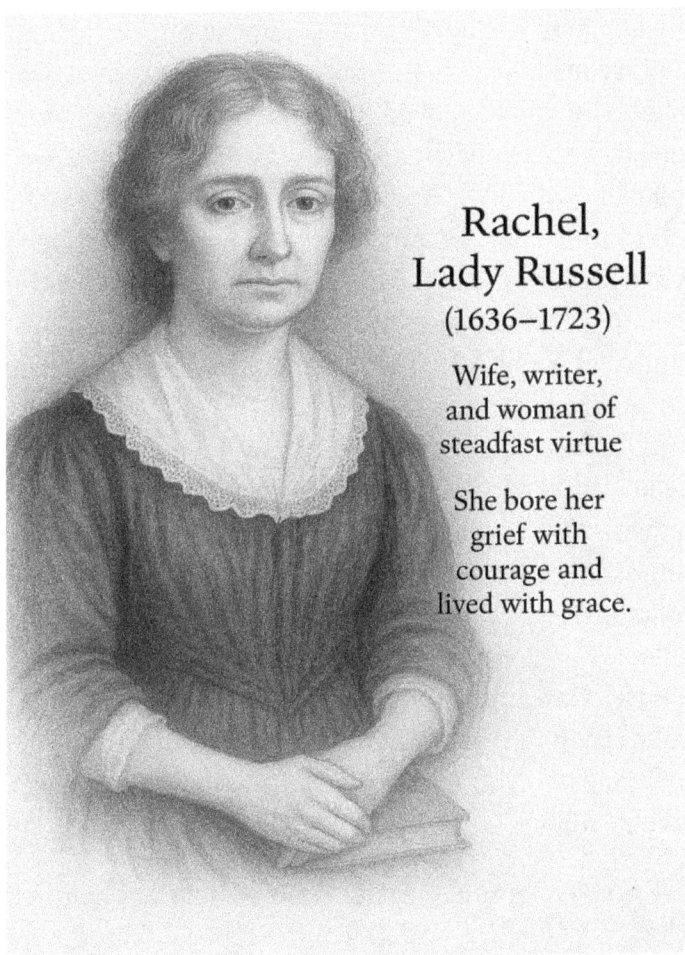

Rachel,
Lady Russell
(1636–1723)

Wife, writer,
and woman of
steadfast virtue

She bore her
grief with
courage and
lived with grace.

Rachel Wriothesley was the daughter of the Earl of Southampton and a French Huguenot lady whom he had married when travelling in France, and who was renowned for her beauty and virtue. Rachel was born in 1636. She never knew her mother, who died when she was an infant. Her father married again, and we know nothing about her relations with her stepmother, but we know that she dearly loved her sisters, and was very good friends with her stepsister. England was passing through troublous times during her childhood on account of the disputes between Charles I. and his Parliament. Lord Southampton was a sensible, moderate man, and he could not approve of the king's doings, but he remained true to him and took his side when the civil war broke out. When the terrible end came and Charles I. was beheaded in 1649, Southampton got permission to watch by the king's body during the night after the execution. He is reported to have told a friend that, whilst he was watching, at about two o'clock in the morning, he heard a step on the stair and a man entered, muffled in a cloak, and stood by the body. He heard him sigh, "Cruel necessity," and knew by the voice that it was Cromwell.

Southampton's moderation was so well known that, though he had been the king's friend, the Parliament did not seize his lands, and he was suffered to live quietly on one of his estates in Hampshire. Rachel was then about thirteen years old and must have benefited from the companionship of her father during these quiet years. We know nothing of her education, and she does not seem in after life to have possessed any learning; but no doubt it was from her father she gained the good sense and the deep religious faith which distinguished her through life. She was an heiress since her father had no son, and only two of his other daughters survived him. As was the custom in those days, a suitable marriage was soon arranged for her. She was only seventeen when she married Lord Vaughan, who died four years afterwards. All that is known of their married life is that Lady Rachel behaved so as to win the love of her husband's family, who always remained her friends. When her husband died, she went to live in Hampshire with her sister Elizabeth, to whom she was deeply attached. Each of the sisters possessed a fine place in Hampshire, and when Elizabeth died both these places, Tichfield and Stratton, belonged to Rachel. Her father had lived to see the restoration of Charles II. and to be one of his first ministers, but he was now dead and Rachel was completely her own mistress. There was no one to arrange a marriage for her, and she was able to choose for herself a man whom she deeply loved. She had known

William Russell, the younger son of the Duke of Bedford, for two years before they were married. He had shown his devotion to her for some time, but perhaps because he was a younger son and she was an heiress, he hesitated at first to ask her to be his wife. They were married at last in 1669, and fourteen years of perfect happiness began for Rachel. The only real sorrow that came to her was the death of her sister, whom she described as "a delicious friend." Her other sorrows were her brief separations from her husband when he had to visit his father at Woburn.

William Russell's elder brother had died, and he was now heir to the dukedom of Bedford. He was not a brilliant man, but he was a very good man, devotedly attached to his family and his friends, and very anxious to do his duty. When they were separated, Lady Russell wrote constantly to him, telling him all she heard that might interest him. When he had only been gone a few hours she wrote that she could not "let this first post night pass, without giving my dear man a little talk." Once, when she had gone over to Tunbridge Wells to drink the waters, she wrote: "After a toilsome day, there is some refreshment to be telling our story to our best friends. I have seen your girl well laid in bed, and ourselves have made our suppers upon biscuits, a bottle of white wine, and another of beer mingled my uncle's way, with nutmeg and sugar. Beds and things are all very well here: our want is yourself and good weather." They had three children, two girls and a boy, and her letters are full of allusions to the eldest: "Our little girl is very well, and extremely merry and often calls Papa. She gets new pretty tricks every day." And another time: "Your girls are very well; Miss Rachel has prattled a long story, but I must omit it. She says Papa has sent for her to Woburn, and then she gallops and says she has been there, and a great deal more."

Lord Russell was in Parliament, but at first he did not take much part in public affairs; he had no ambition and liked his quiet home life better than the bustle of public life. For many years he sat silent in Parliament but his strong love of liberty and of the Protestant religion at last drove him to be more active. There was much discontent with the government of Charles II. and with the favour which he showed to the Roman Catholics. Lord Russell joined himself with a number of others, to whom the nickname of Whigs was given, who were anxious to maintain the rights of Parliament, and to prevent the king's brother James, Duke of York, who was a Roman Catholic, from being considered the heir to the throne. Lady Russell was very anxious lest her husband should do or say anything rash, and even once sent him a little note to the House of Parliament begging him to be silent. People were then very excited and very bitter against those who thought differently from them. An impostor, named Titus Oates, pretended to have discovered a popish plot to destroy the king, and by his false accusations caused many innocent men to be put to death. A few years afterwards, others pretended to have discovered a Whig plot to kill Charles II. and his brother. Lord Russell had not joined in any of the violent accusations made against those opposed to him, nor had he been aware of any plot, but he was a man of great influence, one of the leaders amongst the Whigs, and he too was anxious to keep James from succeeding to the throne. When people were angry and alarmed at the supposed Whig plot, the king and his friends thought it a good opportunity to get rid of some of the Whig leaders. There was one amongst them, Lord Howard, who was ready to secure his own safety by betraying the others. Lord Russell knew that he was in danger, and one day a man was set at his front gate to watch and prevent his going out. But there was no one at his back gate so that he could easily have escaped had he wished. This was perhaps what his enemies wanted. But he felt that to escape would be the same thing as confession of his guilt. He sent his wife out to ask the opinion of his friends, and they agreed with him. So he stayed quietly at home, and the next day he was fetched to appear before the King's Council, and was afterwards sent as a close prisoner to the Tower. He knew the fury of his enemies, and said to his servant that "they would have his life;" and when the servant answered that he hoped they would not have the power, he said, "Yes, the devil is loose."

From that moment, Lord Russell allowed himself no hope. He looked upon himself as a dying man, and turned his thoughts away from this world to another world. But his friends, of course, were eager to do everything to save him. We can imagine what the suffering of his wife must have been; she who had found it hard to bear a separation of a few days, had now to face the terrible probability that he would be condemned to death for high treason. Her first letter to him in the Tower was sent concealed in a cold chicken. Afterwards she seems to have been able to communicate with him more easily. Her courage was equal to her love, and she set to work at once to try to collect evidence in his favour. Her efforts never ceased during the fortnight which passed before he was brought to trial, and she got hold of every possible fact that could be urged in his defence. Moreover, she was brave and self-controlled enough to determine to be present at his trial. She wrote to ask his leave saying: "Your friends believing I can do you some service at your trial, I am extremely willing to try; my resolution will hold out—pray let yours. But it may be the court will not let me; however, do you let me try." When Lord Russell was brought before the Bar at the Old Bailey, he asked for pen, ink, and paper, and the use of the papers that he had, and said, "May I have somebody to write to help my memory?" He was told that he might have one of his servants to write for him, and he answered, "My wife is here, my lord, to do it." The Lord Chief Justice said, "If my lady please to give herself the trouble." So Lady Russell was allowed to be at his side to help him. He was accused of conspiring against the king's life, and of plotting to raise a rebellion in England. Both these accusations he firmly denied. The witnesses against him were men of despicable character and there is no doubt that their evidence was false; but the jury found him guilty, and he was condemned to death as a traitor.

There was only a week left before he was to be executed. His wife and his friends could not give up hope. His father offered the king £50,000 if he would spare his life, and begged him not to bring his grey hairs in sorrow to the grave. People of all kinds interceded with Charles, but it was all in vain. Lady Russell never ceased her efforts. It was suggested that she should try to surprise the king in the park and throw herself at his feet, but this does not seem to have been possible. At her earnest entreaty Lord Russell wrote to the king asking his pardon for having been present at any meetings which may have been unlawful or provoking to the king. But Charles never hesitated. He seems to have regarded Lord Russell as a dangerous person. Lord Russell himself was absolutely resigned to his fate, and only wished to be left in peace to prepare for his death. Every day he was visited by a clergyman, Dr. Burnet, who has left an account of his last days, and Lady Russell was also much with him. She did not distress him by her lamentations, but showed a greatness of spirit which was an immense comfort to him. Sometimes when he spoke of her, the tears would come into his eyes and he would quickly change the subject. Once he said that he wished she would give up beating every bush for his preservation. But he realised that it would help her afterwards to think that she had done everything in her power, just as it helped her during those sad days to have something to do. He was always cheerful and ready to talk and even joke with those who came to see him, but he gave his mind chiefly to prayer and religious thoughts, and to preparing a statement of his opinions which he wished to be distributed after his death. On the last evening of his life, he signed this paper and sent it to be printed. Then some of his friends and his children came to see him, and he was calm and cheerful with his children as usual. He bade his wife stay to supper with him, saying, "Stay and sup with me, let us eat our last earthly food together." He talked cheerfully during supper on various subjects, and particularly of his two daughters. When a note was brought to Lady Russell with some new plan for his deliverance, he turned it into ridicule, so that those who were with him were amazed. At ten o'clock Lady Russell had to leave him. He kissed her four or five times, and she, brave to the last, kept her sorrow so within herself that she gave him no disturbance by their parting. After she was gone, he said, "Now the bitterness of death is past," and he talked long about the blessing she had been to him, and what a comfort it was that in spite of her great tenderness she had never wished him to do a base thing in order to save his life. He said, "What a week should I have passed, if she had been crying on me to turn informer and be a Lord Howard." He thanked God for giving him such a wife, and said that it was a great comfort to him that he left his children in such a mother's hands, and that she had promised to him to take care of herself for their sakes. Then he turned to think of the great change that was before him, and at last went to bed and slept soundly. Those who were with him next morning were amazed at the temper he was in. He thanked God that there was no sort of fear nor hurry in his thoughts, and so he prayed and waited till they came to take him in his coach to his execution. He was still cheerful as he went, singing softly a psalm to himself. As they came near his own house and then turned from it into another street, he said, "I have often turned to the other hand with great comfort, and now I turn to this with greater." But as he looked towards his house, some tears were seen to fall from his eyes. So he remained calm and cheerful till he laid his head on the block and all his troubles were over.

We do not know and we can hardly bear to think how his wife passed those terrible hours after she had parted from him. Seven years afterwards she wrote: "There was something so glorious in the object of my biggest sorrow, I believe, that in some measure kept me from being then overwhelmed." She was roused, only a few days after Lord Russell's death, to defend his memory, since it was asserted that the paper which he had written before his death, and which had been printed and widely read, was not his but had been written by Dr. Burnet. She wrote to the king describing herself as a woman "amazed with grief," and begged him to believe that "he who in all his life was observed to act with the greatest clearness and sincerity, would not at the point of death do so false a thing as to deliver for his own what was properly not so." Still Dr. Burnet was regarded with such suspicion that he thought it wise to leave the country for a time.

Lord William Russell taking leave of his Children previous to his Execution , 1683. (After J. Bridges.)

Lady Russell left London and went with her children to Woburn, the place of the Duke of Bedford, her father-in-law. She had kind friends to help her in her sorrow. The Duke of Bedford cherished her and her children with tender affection, and for long she made her home with him. He addressed her in his letter as his "dearest daughter," and signed himself "your most affectionate father and friend." A clergyman, Dr.

Fitzwilliam, who had been her father's chaplain and had known her from infancy, wrote often to her, and to him she poured out her sorrow, as to one who had known both her and her husband and had seen their life together and therefore would be patient with her whilst her "disordered thoughts" and her "amazed mind" made it difficult for her to speak of anything but her grief. She had promised her husband that she would live for her children, and to their care she now devoted herself, determining to teach them herself, and we do not hear that her daughters ever had any other teacher. Mr. Hoskins, her lawyer, helped her in the management of her affairs with most tender sympathy, and tried to persuade her by degrees to take some interest in them, so that she might not be too entirely absorbed in her sorrow. He told her that great persons had great trials, but also had more opportunity than common people to fit their minds to bear them.

Her children were too young to know what they had lost, and she was determined to do all in her power for them, and particularly for her son, that he might not feel, if he grew to be a man, that it would have been better for him had he had a mother "less ignorant or less negligent." She said that she had no choice in any matter for herself, and could not like one way better than another, so long as what was done was for the good of those young creatures whose service was all the business she had in the world. But she hardly realised how dear her children were to her, till the serious illness of her little boy showed her what it would cost her to part with him. When he recovered she felt that she had indeed something still to live for, and that she might be blessed with some joy and satisfaction through her children. Her little boy was heir to his grandfather, the Duke of Bedford, and on all matters connected with his education she consulted the duke. Neither of them wished to make him begin study too soon, but Lady Russell was anxious that he should have a French tutor, that he might learn the language. There were many Huguenots in England, who had fled from the persecutions in France, and by engaging one of them she was able both to do a charity and to be of use to her son.

Only two years after Lord Russell's execution Charles II. had died and been succeeded by his brother, James II. James II.'s attempt to upset the authority of Parliament, and to rule by his own will alone, led to the rebellion which, in 1688, made his daughter, Mary, and her husband, William of Orange, King and Queen of England. Whilst these stirring events were passing, Lady Russell was living quietly in the country, her only fear was lest her children should run any risk.

Once things were settled, she knew that she could count upon the friendship of William and Mary, and at the Duke of Bedford's wish, she went with him to London. She was full of thankfulness for the change, and wrote that it was difficult to believe that it was more than a dream, yet it was real and an amazing mercy. Her husband's friend, Dr. Burnet, came over with Mary, and was made Bishop of Salisbury. One of the first acts of the new government was to reverse the sentence passed on Lord Russell, and the House of Commons decreed that his execution had been a murder.

Lady Russell was now in a position of influence and importance, but she did not change her quiet way of living. A paper that she wrote about this time for her children shows her loving anxiety for them. In it, after bidding them never to forget their prayers morning and evening, she tells them about her own prayers, and how she always carried with her a little piece of paper on which she noted her faults, that she might ask forgiveness for them; in this way she had gained a habit of constant watchfulness.

One of her anxieties had been to arrange suitable marriages for her children, and it was a great joy to her when her husband's closest friend, the Duke of Devonshire, proposed that his son should marry her eldest daughter. When this marriage was decided on, Lady Elizabeth was only fourteen and Lord Cavendish not sixteen. Lady Russell had to go to London to make the necessary arrangements, and felt it right to go more into society, though she said that going to parties was hard for one with a heavy and weary mind. The marriage was delayed by the bride having an attack of measles, and when it did take place, the young couple only spent three weeks together under Lady Russell's care, and then Lord Cavendish was sent to finish his education by travelling on the continent for two years. A few years later Lady Russell married her younger daughter to the eldest son of the Duke of Rutland, the best match in England. When her son was only fifteen, a seat in Parliament was offered her for him, but she refused because she thought him too young. She had, however, already arranged a marriage for him to a girl in whose education she took the deepest interest. He was married when he was fifteen, but his wife stayed at home with her mother and he went to Oxford for a year's study, during which his mother often visited him. At seventeen he was sent to travel abroad, as Lady Russell believed that to "live well in the world, it is for certain necessary to know the world well." During his travels he caused her some anxiety for he took to gambling, and lost so much money that when he came home, she had to ask his grandfather for money to pay his debts. Shortly afterwards his grandfather died, and he became Duke of Bedford. Now it seemed as if Lady Russell's anxieties were over, since her three children were all happily married, but sorrow followed her to the last. Her son, in the fulness of life and health, was seized with smallpox, the haunting terror of those days before vaccination was discovered. His wife and children had to fly from the infection, and only his mother, with her never-failing courage, stayed to soothe his last moments. Shortly afterwards her younger daughter, the Duchess of Rutland, died. Once again a demand was made on Lady Russell's courage. Her only remaining daughter, the Duchess of Devonshire, had just given birth to a child; it was feared that, if she heard of the death of her sister, the shock might be fatal; so her mother stayed with her and did not let her learn the truth, telling her that she had that day seen her sister out of bed, by which she really meant that she had seen her in her coffin.

Another trouble of Lady Russell's later life was the fear of blindness; but she bore this calamity with patience till an operation restored her sight. She lived till the age of eighty-eight, when she died after a short illness, watched over by the loving care of her only remaining child. During a long life, her courage, her love, her faith had never failed her in spite of her sore trials. It is interesting to remember that three of the chief families of England, the houses of Devonshire, Bedford, and Rutland, look back to this pure, warm-hearted woman and her murdered husband as their common ancestors.

CHAPTER VI
Elizabeth Fry

··· ✦ ···

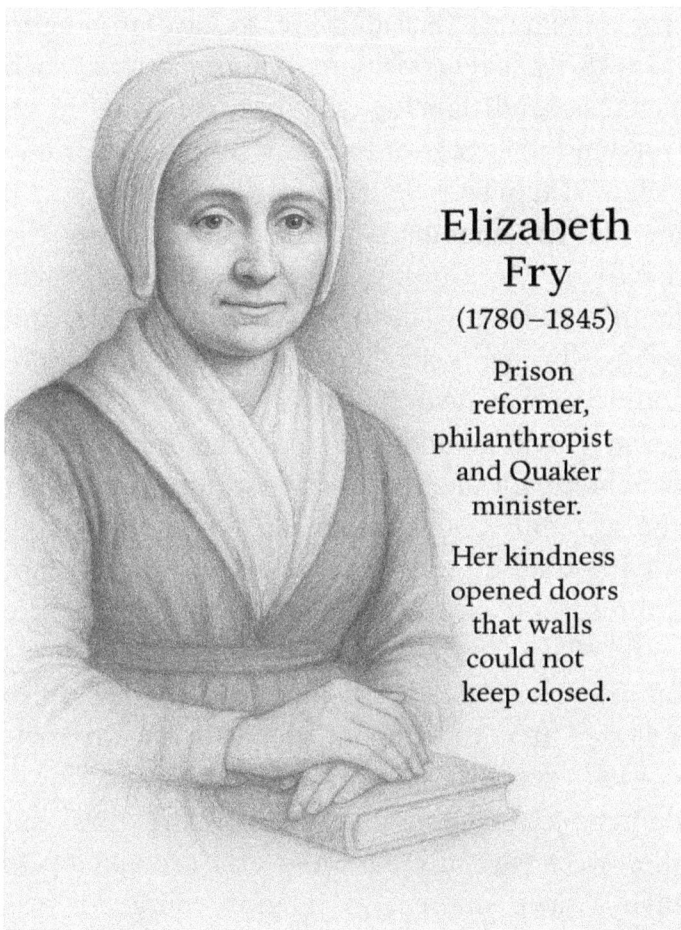

Elizabeth Fry
(1780–1845)

Prison reformer, philanthropist and Quaker minister.

Her kindness opened doors that walls could not keep closed.

In and round Norwich have gathered for a long time many of the chief families belonging to the Society of Friends, the religious body whose members are commonly called Quakers. It was founded by an earnest Christian preacher in the seventeenth century, who taught men to lead a true and simple Christian life, to have nothing to do with what he considered vain pleasures, such as music and dancing, to dress very simply, to worship in silence without any set prayers or any ordained minister, waiting for the Spirit to move one of the members to pray or address the meeting. The Gurneys were one of the chief families belonging to the Society of Friends; and John Gurney, who lived at Earlham, a nice country place near Norwich, was the father of seven daughters and four sons. The third of these daughters, Elizabeth, was born in 1780, and when she was only twelve years old her mother died, leaving Catherine, the eldest child, who was not quite seventeen, to take her place as well as she could. The Gurneys were a very happy, lively family. They did not follow the Quaker rules strictly; they rode about the country on their ponies, dressed in scarlet habits, and loved dancing and singing and gaiety of all kinds. But they were carefully educated and brought up to take a deep interest in religion. Elizabeth was delicate, and could not study much; neither did she often go to Meeting, as the Friends call their religious gathering, partly because she was not strong, and partly because it bored her. One day, when she was eighteen, she had gone to Meeting wearing some very smart boots, which pleased her very much; they were purple, laced with scarlet. She was restless and sat and looked at her boots. But presently a stranger began to preach, a visitor from America. She was forced to listen, and was so moved with what she heard that she began to weep. This was the beginning of a great change in her; she awoke to the reality of religion, and began to feel that she must become what was called a plain Friend, one who followed the rules of the Society in every particular. But first she wished to know more of the world, and, with her father's consent, she paid a visit to London, where she shared in a great deal of gaiety. Still her determination to give it all up only grew stronger. Her sisters, though they dearly loved her, did not share her ideas, and grieved when she would not join their amusements. She found some satisfaction in teaching poor children in Norwich, for whom there were no schools in those days. At last many of her difficulties were settled by her marriage, when she was twenty, with Mr. Joseph Fry, who was also a plain Friend. His family were so strict that amongst her new relations Elizabeth found herself the gay one of the family, instead of the strict one as she had been in her own home.

The Frys lived in London, in the city, as business men then did; later they lived also at Plasket House in Essex, then a beautiful country place, but now covered by the crowded population of East Ham. They had a large family, eleven children in all, and Mrs. Fry was devoted to her husband and her children, but from the first she did not feel that on their account she must give up all work for others. She visited the poor and helped the suffering wherever she could. She was naturally timid and unwilling to put herself forward. Amongst Friends it is the constant habit to trust to the guidance of the Holy Spirit to show both what should be done and to gain strength to do it. As a young woman Mrs. Fry had felt shy even at reading the Bible at family prayers in her own house. As she grew older she began to feel that it might be her duty to speak at the Friends' Meetings. She seemed at last to be driven by the Holy Spirit to do so, and though frightened beforehand, when once she had begun all was easy. The Meeting which she attended was pleased with her speaking and chose her for one of their regular ministers. This was when she was thirty-one and already the mother of seven children. After this she was a frequent speaker at Friends' Meetings all over the country.

The Friends as a body were always anxious to help suffering and misery of every kind. Some gentlemen well known to Mrs. Fry, having learnt of the miserable condition of the women in Newgate, then one of the chief prisons in London, asked her to visit them one winter to see if she could not do something to improve their condition. It was a terrible scene that Mrs. Fry found when, alone with one other lady, she entered Newgate prison in January 1813. In four rooms were crowded nearly 300 women and with them many children. Those who had been tried, and those who had not yet been tried, were all herded together, whether guilty of grave or trifling crimes. There was no woman to take care of them; day and night they were under the charge of one man and his son. They had no employment of any kind; they had no clothing supplied but what they had on when they came. In rags and dirt they slept on the filthy floor without any bedding, and they cooked, lived, and slept in the same rooms. When strangers visited them, as seems to have been allowed, they all started begging, and when they were given any money they at once bought drink, which could be got in the prison. Their language and their conduct were alike terrible, and the governor of the prison himself feared to go amongst them. He begged Mrs. Fry and her companion to remove the watches which hung at their sides lest they should be snatched from them by the women, but they paid no heed to his warning. The two ladies had brought with them a supply of warm garments which they distributed amongst the wretched prisoners, and before leaving each said a few words of prayer, which moved some of their listeners to tears.

Mrs. Fry did not forget what she had seen at Newgate, but it was four years before she was able to do anything more for the prisoners. She was much taken up with family affairs, and she was often ill. She had her own large family, and besides her many brothers and sisters, most of them with families of their own, who all wished her to share their joys and troubles. She was devoted in her care of her children, nursed them when they were ill, and was so gentle and loving in her ways that all little children loved her; but the cares of a large household were burdensome to her and she was glad to give over the management of the house to her daughters as they grew old enough. At Christmas 1816, she again visited Newgate, and this time she asked to be left alone with the women for some hours. She read to them out of the Bible and explained what she had read. The children of the wretched women, half-naked and pining for want of proper food and exercise, especially called forth her pity. She spoke to the mothers about the terrible dangers of their growing up in such a place, and said that if they were willing to help, she would get permission to start a school for the children. The mothers agreed with tears of joy. The governor of the prison had not much hope that anything would come of the experiment, but he agreed to allow an empty cell to be used as a school. A teacher was found amongst the prisoners, a young woman, Mary Connor, who was in prison for stealing a watch. Next day the school was opened, and so many wished to learn that room could not be found for all in the cell. For fifteen months Mary Connor taught the prison school with much devotion; then she was given a free pardon, but died of consumption shortly afterwards. Mrs. Fry and a little group of ladies, whom she interested in the work, helped her constantly. One of these described her first visit to the prison by saying that she felt as if she were going into a den of wild beasts. The half-naked women begging at the top of their voices, struggled together to get to the front of the railing which divided the room. The ladies as they passed through to the school were horrified at the conduct of these poor women, who spent their time in gambling, betting, swearing, fighting, singing, and dancing.

At first it seemed as if the only thing that could be done would be to choose out the least vicious and to try, by keeping them apart, to bring them to a better life. No one thought it possible to do anything for the most degraded. But Mrs. Fry, as she talked with them and got to know them, could not give up hope of being able in some way to be of use to all. She wanted at least to teach them some sort of work; but the officers of the prison assured her that they would only destroy or steal any materials she might give them. Still she was determined to find a way, and a few weeks afterwards she wrote: "A way has very remarkably been opened for us, beyond all expectations, to bring into order the poor prisoners." She was able to form a small association of ladies for the "improvement of the female prisoners at Newgate," and the city magistrates gave her permission to introduce order and work into the prison if it could be done. She and her fellow-workers made their plans, and drew up a set of rules for the life of those prisoners who had been tried. They then gathered the women together, told them what they intended to do for them, and read the rules one by one to them, asking whether they would keep them. All held up their hands in sign of approval after each rule was read, and in the same way they chose monitors amongst themselves to see that the rules were kept. Each day, before work was begun, one of the ladies read the Bible and prayed with the women. All went on so smoothly and well that every one was amazed. After six months, the untried prisoners begged that they too might have work provided for them, which was done.

By degrees, in spite of her desire to keep it quiet, people all over the country began to hear of the work that Mrs. Fry was doing at Newgate, and wrote to ask her advice to help them to improve the condition of other prisons. The House of Commons was led to take interest in the state of the prisons, and invited Mrs. Fry to tell what she knew about them to a committee chosen to look into the matter. It was not only the bad condition of the prisons that troubled her, but the nature of the law, which then punished with death, not only as at present the crime of murder, but also forgery and various kinds of stealing. Mrs. Fry saw many women condemned to death, and was specially troubled by the case of one young woman who had passed some forged notes at the request of the man she loved. She tried in vain to obtain her pardon; and her fate determined her not to rest until the law were changed.

In those days persons guilty of serious crime, who were not condemned to death, were sent as convicts to some of the distant colonies. They were taken to the docks through the streets in open waggons, shouting to the crowd as they passed and behaving with the utmost disorder. This, too, Mrs. Fry set herself to change. She asked that the women might be taken in covered carriages, and promised them that if they would behave quietly she and some of the ladies would come to see them off. Her own carriage followed the long line of coaches which took the women, 128 in number, with their children to the docks. When she reached the ship she was dismayed at the miserable arrangements made for the convicts, who were herded together with no one to care for them and nothing to do. She succeeded in dividing them into classes of twelve with a monitor to keep order over each, and found a corner of the ship where a school could be arranged for the children, with one of the convicts as teacher. To get occupation for the women she collected great quantities of scraps of cloth of all kinds, and set them to make patchwork quilts, which she heard would easily be sold in the colonies. In this way they were able to earn a little money to help them when they came to settle in a new land. She gave Bibles and prayer-books to the monitors for the use of their classes, and made arrangements for those who wished, to learn to read. When the day came for the ship to sail, Mrs. Fry was there to say a last good-bye. She stood at the door of the cabin with her friends and the captain; the women were gathered in front of her, many of the sailors had climbed into the rigging so as to see better what was going on, even the crews in neighbouring ships leant over the sides to watch. Mrs. Fry opened her Bible and amidst profound silence read some verses in her beautiful clear voice. Then she paused for a moment, knelt down on the deck and prayed for God's blessing, whilst many of the women wept. After this a boat carried her to the shore, and the women strained their eyes to see her as long as possible.

Mrs. Fry Reading to the Prisoners in Newgate, 1816.
(After the Picture by Jerry Barrett.)

Mrs. Fry's work at Newgate was talked about everywhere. People of all kinds—bishops, ministers of religion, great nobles, and smart ladies, even members of the royal family—came to Newgate to hear Mrs. Fry teach and pray with the prisoners. It became a fashionable amusement, but the solemn scene could not fail to affect even the most frivolous. As they listened to Mrs. Fry's winning voice, with its beautiful silvery tones, they forgot to think of the prisoners and thought only of the way in which the words she had spoken touched their own lives. The silence that followed used to be broken by sobs from prisoners and visitors alike.

Mrs. Fry gave her mind not only to teaching the prisoners and trying to lessen their sufferings, but to studying the whole question of prison reform. She wished to see things so changed that prisons might become places where criminals should not only be punished but helped to become better. She travelled all over the country, sometimes with her husband, sometimes with her brothers, who were also zealous workers in prison reform, visiting the different prisons. Journeys were sometimes undertaken also to visit Friends' Meetings and speak at them; but wherever she went she always tried to inspect the prison, to form ladies' committees to visit the prisons, and to persuade the authorities to improve their arrangements. She tried to be of use to other people also. There was a great deal of smuggling in those days, and there had to be many stations of coastguards to watch for smugglers. Mrs. Fry was sorry for the dull and lonely lives led by many of these men, and with the help of her friends provided for their use libraries of books at all the coastguard stations.

She went to Ireland also to visit the prisons with her brother, who was deeply interested in the same work, and later they visited Jersey. Whenever she was in London, she paid a weekly visit to Newgate, and she sometimes visited the men as well as the women. The Prime Minister, Lord Melbourne, was full of admiration for her work, and helped her to get improvements made in the care of the women and children on the convict ships.

Mrs. Fry's fame had spread over Europe, and when she was already fifty-nine, with many grandchildren growing up around her, she decided to visit France and study French prisons. Wherever she went she was received with much enthusiasm. Some of the prisons that she saw she admired very much, but in others she noticed much to criticise, and she always freely expressed her opinions. In some towns in France she was able to form committees of ladies to visit the prisons. After a second visit she prepared a long report for the French government about the prisons she had seen, and the reforms she thought desirable. Repeated requests came to her to visit new places, and she made a third journey to the continent with her brother, when they got as far as Berlin. In Prussia she was treated with much honour by the king and queen, and by many members of the royal family. The following year the King of Prussia came to England, and one of the things he was most anxious to do whilst in London was to be present at one of Mrs. Fry's visits to Newgate. He came to the prison accompanied by the Lord Mayor and many gentlemen. There in one of the wards Mrs. Fry and some of the ladies were gathered with about sixty of the poor women. She told them that the presence of such distinguished visitors must not be allowed to distract their attention, and she read the Bible and prayed with them as usual. The same day the king drove out to see her at her own house in the country, and she presented to him her large family, sons and daughters, with their wives and twenty-five grandchildren. She writes of the day: "Our meal was handsome and fit for a king, yet not extravagant, everything most complete and nice. I sat by the king, who appeared to enjoy his dinner, perfectly at his ease and very happy with us."

Once more after this Mrs. Fry visited France, but she was growing feeble and tired out with her many labours. She had to suffer some months of illness, during which her daughters tended her with the greatest devotion. She wrote herself that she was much struck in this illness with the manner in which her children had been raised up as her helpers. Many sorrows came to her in her last years from the death of her relations, but suffering and sorrow did not shake her faith. She had the comfort during the last years of her life, of hearing of all the improvements that were being made in the prisons, to reform which she had done so much. To the last she shared all the joys and sorrows of her children and of the other members of her large family. For about two years she led more or less the life of an invalid, and died in October 1845, at the age of sixty-five.

It has only been possible to tell a very little of all the work she did for others during the years of her busy life. But whilst she did all this public work, and influenced kings and governments in favour of reforms, and ministered herself to the needs of the sinful and the suffering, she never forgot her duties as a devoted wife and the mother of a large family of children, who loved her with the deepest tenderness. Neither did she neglect her brothers and sisters and their children. Her public work, though it absorbed much time and thought, did not take her away from her other duties. She remains an example of what a woman can do who feels the call to serve others, and who does not believe that she can refuse to obey that call even though she has a family and a husband to care for.

CHAPTER VII

Mary Somerville

... ✧ ...

Mary Somerville
(1780–1872)

Scientist, writer, and pioneer of women's education.

She showed that the mind, like the stars, shines brightest in freedom.

Mary Fairfax, who grew up to be the most learned woman of her day, was born in Scotland in 1780. Her father was a captain in the navy, and whilst he was away with his ship, her mother, who was not at all well off, lived quietly with her children at Burntisland, a small seaport on the coast of Fife. She did not take much trouble about Mary's education. In those days it was not thought necessary that girls should learn much; Mary was taught to read the Bible and to say her prayers morning and evening, but otherwise was allowed to grow up a wild creature. As a little girl of seven or eight she pulled the fruit for preserving, shelled the peas and beans, fed the poultry, and looked after the dairy. She did not care for dolls, and had no one to play with her, for her only brother was some years older; but she was very happy in the garden, and loved to watch the birds and learnt to know them by their flight.

When her father came home from sea, he was shocked to find Mary, who was then nearly nine years old, such a savage. She had not yet been taught to write, but she used to read the "Arabian Nights," "Robinson Crusoe," and the "Pilgrim's Progress." He was horrified too at her strong Scotch accent, and made her read aloud to him that he might correct it. This she found a great trial, but she delighted in helping her father in the care of his garden, to which he was devoted. He at last felt that something more must be done to educate her, and said to her mother: "Mary must at least know how to write and keep accounts." So at ten years old she was sent to a boarding school. The change from her wild, free life made her wretched, and she spent her days in tears. They were very particular in those days that a girl's figure should be straight, and used strange means to ensure this. Mary was perfectly straight and well-made, but she was enclosed in stiff stays with a steel busk; bands were fastened over her frock to make her shoulder-blades meet at the back, and a sort of steel collar was put under her chin, supported on a rod which was fastened to the busk in her stays. Under these uncomfortable conditions, she and the other girls of her age had to do their lessons. These lessons were far from interesting. The chief thing she had to do was to learn by heart a page of Johnson's Dictionary, so as to be able, not only to spell all the words and give their meaning, but to repeat the page quickly. She also learnt to write, and was taught a little French and English grammar.

A year at this school was supposed to finish her education, and it is not surprising that when she got home again at the age of eleven, she could not write a tidy letter. She was reproached with not having profited better by the money spent on keeping her at an expensive school; her mother said that she would have been content had she only learnt to write well and to keep accounts, as that was all a woman was expected to know. Mary was delighted to be free again, and felt like a wild animal escaped out of a cage. She spent hours on the seashore studying the shells and the stones, and watching the crabs and jelly-fish. When bad weather kept her indoors, she read every book she could find, and especially delighted in Shakespeare, but an aunt who visited them found fault with her mother for letting her spend so much time in reading, and she was sent to the village school to learn plain sewing. She soon made a fine linen shirt for her brother so well that she was taken away from school and given the charge of all the house linen, which she had to make and to mend. But she was vexed that people should find fault with her reading, and thought it unjust that women should have been given a desire for knowledge, if it were wrong for them to acquire it. Every opportunity for study was used by her, and when a cousin lent her a French book, she set to work, with the help of a dictionary and the little grammar she had learnt at school, to make out the sense of it. There were two small globes in the house, and her mother allowed the village schoolmaster to come during a few weeks in the winter evenings to teach her how to use them. She loved to watch the stars from her bedroom window, and to find out their names on the celestial globe.

When Mary was thirteen, her mother spent a winter in Edinburgh, and then at last Mary went to a school where she learnt a little arithmetic and to write properly. An uncle gave her a piano, and she had lessons in playing it. When they got back to Burntisland she used to spend four or five hours daily at her piano. She also began to teach herself Latin, but did not dare to tell this to any one till she went to stay with an uncle who was very kind to her. She told him what she was doing, and he encouraged her by telling her about learned women in the past, and what was more, read Virgil with her in his study every morning for an hour or two. Whilst staying with another uncle in Edinburgh, she attended a dancing school, and learnt to dance minuets and reels. Party politics were violent in those days, and Mary's father and uncle were strong Tories. She heard such bitter abuse of the Liberals that her sense of justice was revolted, and she adopted Liberal opinions, which she stuck to all her life.

Mary Fairfax was probably about fifteen when one day a friend showed her a monthly magazine containing coloured pictures of ladies' dresses and puzzles. She was surprised to see strange lines mixed up with letters in the puzzles in a way that she could not understand, and asked her friend what they were. She was told that they were a kind of arithmetic called algebra, but her friend could not tell her what algebra was. On going home she looked amongst the family books to see if there was one which would explain algebra. She could only find one about navigation, which she studied, though she could but dimly understand it. She had no one of whom she could ask questions, and knew that she would only be laughed at if she spoke of her desire for knowledge, so that she often felt sad and forlorn. But she managed to teach herself enough Greek to read Xenophon and Herodotus. The next winter she spent in Edinburgh again and was sent to a drawing school, and got on well with drawing; but it was not till the following summer, when her youngest brother was studying with a tutor, that she ventured to ask the tutor to get her books about algebra and Euclid, and she was able to begin the studies which were to make her famous as a mathematician. She worked very hard, for she had many household duties to perform, and to spend much time on music and painting, which were the only studies of which her mother approved. She could only study mathematics by sitting up late at night, and burnt so many candles that the servants complained to her mother, and her candle was ordered to be taken away when she went to bed. Then she used to keep up her studies by going over in the dark what she had already learnt.

By this time Mary was grown up, and was a remarkably pretty girl, very small and delicate-looking. She began to go out to parties in Edinburgh, which she much enjoyed, and where she was much admired; but all the time she never lost sight of what she felt to be the main object of her life, the pursuit of her studies. She painted at the art school, she practised her piano for five hours every day, she made all her own dresses, even her ball dresses, she spent her evenings working and talking with her mother. To get time for her other studies, she used to rise at daybreak, and, after dressing, wrapt herself in a blanket to keep warm, and read algebra or classics till breakfast time. So amidst difficulties of all kinds she struggled on with her studies; no one, except her uncle Dr. Somerville, ever gave her any help or encouragement.

When she was twenty-four, Mary Fairfax married her cousin, Samuel Grieg, and went to live in London. Her husband was out at his work all day and she had plenty of time for her studies. But though he did not interfere with what she did, he gave her no help or encouragement. He knew nothing of science himself, and did not believe that women were capable of intellectual work. She struggled on as best she could and took lessons in French so as to learn to speak it. After three years her husband died, leaving her with two little boys, one of whom did not live to grow up. Mary went back to live with her parents; she cared for her children with the utmost tenderness, but she still devoted herself to her mathematical studies, and she was able to get advice and help from a professor in Edinburgh. To get time to study she still rose early, for during most of the day she was busy with her children, and the evening she devoted to her father. People thought her queer and foolish, because she did not go into society; but she did not care for their criticisms, and made real progress in her studies.

She had several proposals of marriage, but refused them all till, in 1812, she agreed to marry her cousin, Dr. William Somerville, son of the uncle who had been the only person to help her in her studies when she was a girl. When her engagement was known, one of Dr. Somerville's sisters, who was younger than herself and unmarried, wrote to her saying she "hoped she would give up her foolish manner of life and studies and make a respectable and useful wife to her brother." This made Dr. Somerville very indignant, and he wrote a severe and angry letter to his sister. After this none of his family dared to interfere with his wife again. His father was delighted with his choice, for he understood and loved his niece. Some of the family were much astonished, when in the summer after the marriage they were staying together in the lakes, and one of them fell ill and expressed a wish for currant jelly, to find that Mrs. Somerville, in spite of her learning, was able at once to make some excellent jelly.

The marriage was an absolutely happy one. Dr. Somerville loved and admired his wife and was very proud of her learning. For the first time she had encouragement to pursue her studies instead of having obstacles thrown in her way. At first they lived in Edinburgh, but, in 1816, Dr. Somerville received an appointment in London, and they moved there and settled in Hanover Square. Many friends gathered round them, and Mrs. Somerville enjoyed intercourse with other learned people, especially with Sir William Herschel, the great astronomer. She not only went on with her scientific studies, but she took lessons in painting. She and her husband enjoyed making together a collection of minerals. They added to it on their travels in France and Italy, which were an immense delight to her. Several children were born to Mrs. Somerville, but only one son of her first marriage and two daughters of her second marriage lived to grow up. She was a devoted mother, and gave much time to the care of her children. She gave her morning hours to domestic duties, and was determined that her daughters should not suffer as she had done from want of a good education. She taught them herself all the subjects she was able to teach, giving three hours to their lessons every morning. Her house was carefully managed, and she used to read the newspapers diligently as she was keenly interested in politics; she read, too, all the most important new books on all kinds of subjects. Science was her special study, but she loved poetry and read all the great authors in Latin and Greek as well as in French and Italian. She was very fond of music and devoted to painting, and was very clever and neat with her needle, and she also enjoyed society very much. Miss Edgeworth, the novelist, after meeting her in 1822, described her as small and slight, with smiling eyes and a charming face, quiet and modest in her ways, with a very soft voice and a pleasant Scotch accent. She said of her: "While her head is among the stars her feet are firm upon the earth."

Mrs. Somerville never herself introduced learned subjects into general talk, but when others did she spoke of them simply, and naturally without assuming any superior knowledge. Yet, of course, other learned people soon found out how much she knew. When she was in Edinburgh, she had written, at the request of the editor, a learned article on comets for the Quarterly Review, but she had no idea of writing any book till, in 1827, a letter came from Lord Brougham to Dr. Somerville asking whether Mrs. Somerville would write, for a series he was interested in, a book on a very important French work about the stars written by the famous astronomer, La Place. Mrs. Somerville had met La Place in Paris; he had said of her that she was the only woman who could understand his works, and Lord Brougham wrote that she was the only person who could write the book he wanted, and if she would not write it, it must be left undone. Mrs. Somerville writes herself that she was surprised beyond expression by this letter. She thought Lord Brougham must be mistaken as to her powers, and that it would be very presumptuous in her "to attempt to write on such a subject or indeed on any other." However, Lord Brougham called in person to press his request, and at last she agreed, on condition that no one should know what she was trying to do, and that if she failed the manuscript should be put into the fire.

She had now to try to make time for more work in her busy life. This she did by getting up earlier to see to her household duties, but she was much disturbed by interruptions. People did not think that a woman was like a man and could have any real work to do. Frequently friends or relations would arrive when she was in the midst of a difficult problem and say, "I have come to spend a few hours with you." She had no other room to work in but the drawing-room, and as soon as the bell warned her of a visitor, she used to cover up her books and papers with a piece of muslin so that no one should know what she was doing. She learnt by habit to put up with interruptions, and to go back at once when alone again, to the point where she had left off. She did her work in the same room where her children prepared their lessons after she had taught them, and she was never impatient when they brought their little difficulties to her, but answered them quickly and quietly and went back to her own work. She could so abstract her mind that even talking or practising on the piano did not disturb her.

When the book was finished and sent to be looked at, Mrs. Somerville felt very nervous as to what might be thought of it. It made her very happy and proud when the great astronomer, Sir John Herschel, wrote to say that he had read it with the highest admiration, and added: "Go on thus and you will leave a memorial of no common kind to posterity; and, what you will value far more than fame, you will have accomplished a

148

most useful work." Her book was received with immense praise. The scientific societies hastened to show her honour; her bust was ordered to be executed by the great sculptor, Chantrey, and placed in the hall of the Royal Society of London, and at the prime minister's request, the king granted her a pension of £200 a year. The relations who had found fault with her ways were now astonished at her success, and were loud in her praise; but most of all she valued the deep delight of her husband, who had always encouraged her, and whose pride in her knew no bounds.

After this success other scientific books were written by Mrs. Somerville. Much of her work was done in Italy, where they went on account of Dr. Somerville's health. In Rome, as in London, Mrs. Somerville never allowed anything to interfere with her morning's work, but in the afternoon she enjoyed keenly going about to see the wonderful sights of the city or making excursions into the country. She wrote to her son in 1841 that she had undertaken a book more fit for the combination of a society than for a single hand to accomplish. This was her book on Physical Geography, with which she was at first so dissatisfied that she wished to burn it. But her husband begged her to send it to Sir John Herschel, who advised that it should be published, and it went through six editions.

In 1860, Mrs. Somerville had the great sorrow of losing her husband, who died in Florence at the age of eighty-nine. One who knew them well and had only lately seen them together, spoke of them as giving the most beautiful instance of united old age. Mrs. Somerville continued to live in Italy with her two daughters, first in Spezzia and afterwards in Naples. To the last she worked on, writing a new book, bringing out new editions of her old books, and working at them so as to include in them the latest scientific discoveries. She used to study in bed every day from eight in the morning till twelve or one o'clock. A little bird, a mountain sparrow, was her constant companion for eight years and would sit and even go to sleep on her arm whilst she wrote. It was a real sorrow when one day it disappeared and was found drowned in a water jug. She still painted, and enjoyed sketching the beautiful view that could be seen from her windows.

Somerville College, Oxford.

In 1869 there was an agitation in England to gain for women the right to vote in Parliamentary elections. Mrs. Somerville thought decidedly that women ought to have the vote and signed petitions for it, and she felt it to be an honour to be put on the General Committee for Woman Suffrage in London. She thought that in many ways the laws were unjust to women, and also that there was still a strong prejudice against the higher education of women. She was much interested in all that was being done in England to improve girls' education, remembering well her own difficulties as a girl, and heard with much delight of the establishment of the women's colleges at Cambridge. After her death one of the first women's colleges at Oxford was named after her, Somerville College. In 1868 she was much interested in a tremendous eruption of Mount Vesuvius, the volcano which she could see from her windows on the other side of the bay of Naples. Day after day she watched with a telescope the glowing streams of lava and the flame and smoke which burst from the mountain, carrying with it great rocks into the air. It was a great pleasure to her to see some distinguished men of science, who came from England to see the eruption, and who spent an evening with her, during which she enjoyed much scientific conversation.

Mrs. Somerville lived to a great old age. When she was ninety her eyesight and the powers of her mind were still perfectly good. She still studied science and the higher mathematics in the early morning hours, afterwards she would read Shakespeare or Dante, or Homer in the original. She regularly read the newspapers, and enjoyed a cheerful novel in the evening, or a game of bezique with her daughters. It was for her a constant joy to watch the sunsets over the bay of Naples: the flowers or seaweeds which her daughters brought in from their walks, or the tame birds she had in her room, were always a delight. She had ever been deeply religious, and everything in nature spoke to her of the great God who had created all things, whilst the laws which were revealed to her in her scientific studies gave her ever new cause to love and adore her heavenly Father. Friends from England and Italy came often to see her, for she was much beloved. Her only infirmity was that she was very deaf; but no one, young or old, thought it a hardship to sit by the little, sweet, frail old lady and tell her about the things that were going on in the world outside in which she still took so keen an interest. Even when she was ninety-two she would drive out sometimes for several hours. She often forgot recent events and the names of people, but she wrote herself at the age of ninety-two: "I am still able to read books on the higher algebra for four or five hours in the morning, and even to solve the problems. Sometimes I find them difficult, but my old obstinacy remains, for if I do not succeed to-day I attack them again on the morrow. I also enjoy reading about all the new discoveries and theories in the scientific world and in all branches of science." She thought much of the last journey that lay before her, but wrote that it did not disturb her tranquillity, for though deeply sensible of her utter unworthiness, she trusted in the infinite mercy of her Almighty Creator. Tended by the loving care of her daughters, she was perfectly happy. Her beautiful life ended in perfect peace and her pure spirit passed away so gently that those around her scarcely perceived that she had left them. She died in her sleep one morning at the age of ninety-two.

CHAPTER VIII

Julia Selina Inglis

··· ✧ ···

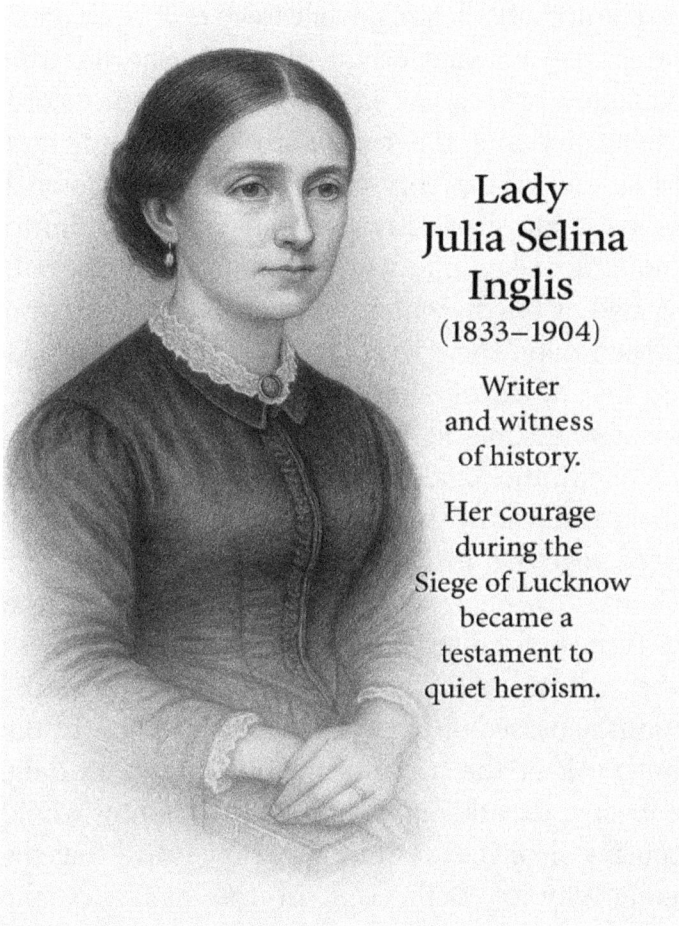

Lady Julia Selina Inglis
(1833–1904)

Writer and witness of history.

Her courage during the Siege of Lucknow became a testament to quiet heroism.

There were many brave Englishwomen in India during the terrible days of the Indian mutiny, many as brave as Mrs. Inglis, but we are able to know what she went through at the time, because of the diary which she kept and in which she wrote down what happened day after day, and in reading about her adventures we can imagine something of what others suffered. She was the daughter of a great lawyer, who became Lord Chancellor and the first Lord Chelmsford, and when she was twenty-eight she married Colonel Inglis, a brave soldier, and went out with him to India. Six years afterwards the mutiny broke out, caused by the discontent of the native troops, who turned upon their English officers. Lucknow was in the heart of the most disaffected district. Lieutenant-Colonel Inglis had gone there with his regiment, the 32nd, in January 1857; his wife and their three little boys were with him, and they lived together in a pleasant little bungalow. Sir Henry Lawrence was the Commissioner, as the governor of a district of India was called. He was very anxious about the state of affairs, and as the months passed and news came to Lucknow of the outbreak of the mutiny in other parts, he daily expected that the native troops in Lucknow would mutiny also. On the 16th May they heard that the great city of Delhi was in the hands of the mutineers. Then Sir Henry Lawrence ordered that the wives and children of the officers at Lucknow should leave their own houses and come into the Residency, the place in the centre of the city where the Commissioner lived, and near which the troops were quartered. This he thought he could defend against the natives if they should mutiny. He invited the ladies belonging to the 32nd regiment to stay in his house that they might be near their husbands.

Mrs. Inglis got herself and her children ready as quickly as possible, and then rode up and down the road outside her house waiting for the officer who was to escort them. It was an hour before Colonel Case arrived with a troop of cavalry. He rode in front and Mrs. Inglis followed on her pony with the other ladies and the children behind them. The city was as quiet as if it were asleep, and they reached Sir Henry Lawrence's house in safety. Mrs. Inglis writes: "I think it was the longest day I ever passed, as, of course, we could settle to nothing. John [her husband] came in the evening and read the service with me; he told me he did not think we should ever return to our house." At dinner she sat next Sir Henry, who was very grave and silent. About 130 English women and children took refuge in the Residency, and were given rooms in the different houses and offices there. In Sir Henry Lawrence's house there were eleven ladies and fifteen children, and in spite of all he had to do, he took endless trouble to make them comfortable. Mrs. Inglis had a small room for herself and her three children. Colonel Inglis had to stay with his soldiers, and she used to drive with her friend Mrs. Case to camp that they might spend a little time each day with their husbands. These visits were a great treat to them, but they had to return before dusk, and even so, driving through the city was not very prudent, as there were many ill-looking men about. Mrs. Inglis drove her pony herself and went at a very good pace. At first she was cheerful enough and inclined to laugh at the absurd reports that reached them, till her husband checked her, saying, "It's no laughing matter, the most dreadful reports reach us daily." From that moment she realised the true seriousness of their position. The very next day she was just going to bed when a gentleman knocked at her door and bade her bring her children and come up to the top of the house immediately. She dressed them as quickly as possible and hurried to the roof and found all the inmates of the house gathered together looking towards the camp where many tires were blazing. The chaplain offered prayer, and the men prepared to defend the position in case they were attacked. At midnight a note came to Mrs. Inglis from her husband, and every one crowded round her to hear the news. He said that for the moment the rising was over, and he did not think that it had been general. Then they all lay down to rest. But at noon the next day, they heard of a rising all over the city, and every one was bidden to come to the Residency for safety. There was terrible confusion and excitement, every one fearing the worst. A few minutes' talk with her husband, who came in the evening, was a great comfort to Mrs. Inglis. She had to share her small room now with her friend Mrs. Case and her sister. Everything possible was done to strengthen their position. About 765 native troops had remained faithful, and they with 927 European troops were quartered in houses all round the Residency, which were connected by a hastily built wall. Many native servants were faithful to their masters, and Mrs. Inglis had a devoted native butler and nurse, who did all they could to help her. Her husband had a little room in the house, so she could see him sometimes for a few minutes, but he was terribly busy. Morning and evening the chaplain read prayers, and every Sunday there were services, which were a great comfort.

On June 13th, Mrs. Inglis asked her husband if he thought the enemy would attack them and if they would be able to hold out. He answered that he believed that they would be attacked, that their position was a bad one, and they would have a hard struggle. She says she was glad to know what to expect, as it enabled her to prepare for the worst. She describes their life as most wearisome. The heat was very great; it was impossible to read much, but they occupied their time in making clothes for the refugees, and this employment was a comfort. She always slept with her children on the roof of the house, and the nights in the open air were very pleasant. The view of the city and the country around was very beautiful, and so calm and peaceful that it was impossible to think it could be the scene of war. Colonel Inglis slept in the garden with the soldiers. Occasionally he managed to come during the day into his wife's room for a few minutes. She never left the house, except once for a walk with the chaplain to see the fortifications. The church was used for service for the last time on June 14th, after that it was turned into a storehouse for grain. Mrs. Inglis herself laid in all the stores she could get, sugar, arrowroot, beer, wine, and food for the goats who supplied milk for the children.

About this time Mrs. Inglis began to feel ill, and it was discovered that she had the smallpox. She wished to be moved to a tent so as not to expose others to infection, but it was decided that the risk would be too great; for it was known that a great force of rebels were approaching the city, and that they would soon be besieged. All the troops in Lucknow were now brought in from the camp and stationed in and about the Residency and a fort near by. Then, on June 30th, some of them were ordered out to meet and drive back the rebels. But the natives with the guns proved faithless and deserted the English, so that the force had to retreat. Mrs. Inglis, ill though she was, could not stay in bed, and posted herself at the window to see the sad sight of the troops straggling back in twos and threes. She and her friend Mrs. Case were in terrible anxiety about their husbands. Just then Colonel Inglis came in; he was crying, and, after kissing his wife, he turned to Mrs. Case and said, "Poor Case." Mrs. Inglis writes that never will she forget the shock of his words, nor the cry of agony from his widow. Colonel Inglis had to leave them at once. In all the horror of the moment there was no time for thought. The rebels were firing heavily on the Residency, and the room was not safe. Hastily collecting a few necessaries, Mrs. Inglis and her children took refuge with the other ladies in a room below, which was almost underground; the shot was flying about so quickly that they could not venture out, and not long after they had left their room upstairs a shell fell into it. Fortunately her native servants were faithful, and brought them food during the day.

The Gateway of the Residency, Lucknow, showing marks of Shot and Shell on the Brickwork.

At night the firing grew less, and Colonel Inglis came in to take them over to a room he had prepared for them in a building which had been the gaol, and which was fairly safe. It was only 12 ft. by 6, and there she and her children stayed with Mrs. Case and her sister. They were all so worn out with wretchedness that they slept that night. Next day they did what they could to make their room comfortable. It had neither doors nor windows, only open arches, and they hung up curtains to make some sort of privacy. Though the smallpox was then at its height, Mrs. Inglis suffered no harm from the anxieties of that terrible day; but she was alarmed lest her children should catch the disease, as she could not keep them from her bed. But fortunately they did not take any harm, and she seems to have recovered quickly. There were two wells in their courtyard, so that they had a plentiful supply of water, and for the moment there was plenty of food.

The next day another terrible attack was made by the rebels. As they sat trembling in the midst of the heavy cannonading, feeling sure that the enemy must get in, Mrs. Case proposed that they should say the litany, which they did, she and her sister kneeling by Mrs. Inglis's bed. Mrs. Inglis writes that the soothing effect was marvellous; they grew calm in spite of their alarm. Next morning Sir Henry Lawrence was wounded by a shell that burst into his room. There was no hope of his recovery, and after three days of awful suffering, nobly borne, he died, leaving the entire command to Colonel Inglis. Day after day one or other of the little garrison or of the women were hit by shells. The chaplain was shot whilst shaving one morning. Mrs. Inglis watched anxiously over her children, who grew pale and thin from the confinement and the terrible heat. July 16th, was her little boy's birthday, and she thought sadly of the other children of his father's regiment who on that day used to have a dinner and a dance in his honour. She did not know that on that very day those other poor children were murdered by the rebels at Cawnpore.

Every day the anxiety grew. They had hoped before this to hear of English troops coming to relieve them, but no news came. There was nothing to be done but to wait and try to keep back the rebels, whose attacks were constant. Death was always near. One evening Mrs. Inglis was standing outside the door with her baby in her arms when she heard something whiz past her ears. She rushed inside, and afterwards found a piece of shell buried in the ground just where she had been standing. Her children were her greatest comfort, and as she had them to amuse and look after she never had an idle moment. Sometimes she tried to read aloud, but it was impossible for them to fix their minds on a book. In their games the children would imitate what was going on around them. They made balls of earth and threw them against the wall saying that they were shells bursting. Johnny, the eldest boy, would hear where a bullet fell and run and pick it up whilst it was still warm. They slept through all the firing and never seemed frightened.

Sunday services were regularly held, and again and again at the worst moments prayer was their only support. Mrs. Inglis used to visit the other ladies as much as she could; and, being of a hopeful nature herself, managed to raise their spirits. Her own best moment in the day was in the early morning, when her husband used to come to see her and sit outside her door drinking his tea. One day a shell burst in their own courtyard; the children were playing about and for a moment her anxiety was intense, till she saw that they were all safe. Tales of hairbreadth escapes were heard daily; one doctor had his pillow under his head shot without his being hurt. But there were many who did not escape and the condition of the wounded in the heat and the crowded hospital left little hope of recovery. Anxiety and constant work turned Colonel Inglis's hair grey during the long suspense. Their position was growing desperate. He knew that General Havelock was trying to fight his way through the rebels and come to their help, for a native spy carried letters between the two commanders, written in Greek characters and rolled up and hidden in a quill. General Havelock wished Colonel Inglis to be ready to help his approach by an attack from inside, but Colonel Inglis was obliged to write on August 16th, after more than six weeks of siege, that this was impossible, owing to the weak condition of his shattered force. Food was growing scarce, and there was much sickness. On one evening five babies were buried.

It was not till near the end of September that the sound of distant guns struck Mrs. Inglis's ear one day and told her that relief was near. Each boom seemed to her to say, "We are coming to save you." Five days afterwards, on September 25th, at six in the evening, she heard tremendous cheering and knew that the relief had come. She was standing outside her door, when a soldier came rushing up to fetch the Colonel's sword, which he had not worn since the siege began. A few minutes afterwards the Colonel himself entered, bringing with him Colonel Havelock, a short grey-haired man. He had fought his way in with the relief force. He shook hands with Mrs. Inglis, saying that he feared she had suffered a great deal. She could hardly speak to answer him, and only longed to be alone with her husband. Colonel Inglis felt the same, and after taking Havelock out, returned in a few minutes, and, kissing her, exclaimed, "Thank God for this." For a brief moment there was unmixed happiness. Then the thought rushed into her mind of all the others whose lot was so different from hers and whose dear ones had perished in the siege.

A moment later a messenger came asking if they had any cold meat for starving officers, and very soon Mrs. Inglis learnt how severely those who had come to their rescue had suffered as they fought their way in through the narrow streets of the town. She also heard of the wonderful scene when they at last got in and met the besieged. On all sides were hand-shakings and warm greetings, the relieving soldiers lifting the children of the besieged in their arms and kissing them. But little by little Mrs. Inglis realised that, though relieved, they were not rescued. The soldiers who had fought their way in under Outram and Havelock were not enough to drive back the enemy or even to take the women and children safely out of Lucknow. They were only able to help them to resist the besiegers, and their presence increased the anxiety about the supply of food, which was getting very low and had to be used with the greatest care. The number of wounded was also terribly increased, and the state of the overcrowded hospital and the want of all the things needed for the care and comfort of the patients added greatly to their suffering. The only chance now was to hold out till the coming of Sir Colin Campbell with more troops, and meanwhile the attacks of the enemy increased in fury; there was constant firing and no place was really safe, so that Mrs. Inglis was never easy if her children were out of her sight.

During the siege, Mrs. Inglis had found a little white hen which used to stay about their room and be fed by her children. When food grew scarce they decided to kill and eat it; but that very morning Johnny ran in exclaiming, "O, mamma, the white hen has laid an egg." One of the officers, whose leg had been cut off, was very ill and weak, and Mrs. Inglis at once took the egg, a great luxury in those days, to him. The hen laid an egg for him every day till he died and then ceased for the rest of the siege, but they would not kill it after that.

It was not till the middle of November, seven weeks after the coming of Havelock, that they knew that Sir Colin Campbell was near. It was Colonel Inglis's birthday, and they invited another officer to dinner, and actually had a fruit tart for dinner, a luxury which Mrs. Inglis would not have dreamt of had not her hope of relief been high. Little Johnny ran out to call their guest, screaming at the top of his voice, "Come to dinner; we've got a pudding."

It was November 17th, a most anxious, exciting day, when Sir Colin Campbell at last reached Lucknow. He did not come inside the entrenchments, and when Colonel Inglis arrived very late to dinner it was with the bad news that they were all to leave the Residency the next evening. Sir Colin did not think he was strong enough to recapture the town, and felt that the utmost he could do was to carry off in safety the garrison and the women and children. It was a bitter blow to Colonel Inglis to be told that he must leave in the hands of the enemy the place which he had so long defended at such terrible loss. He offered to stay and hold it if 1000 men could be left to him and the women and children removed; but it was not allowed, and there was nothing to do but to obey. There was a hurried packing of all such things as could be taken with them. The women and children started, late on the afternoon of November 19th, to leave the place where they had been closely besieged for nearly five months. The road by which they were led out of the town was considered safe, except in three places on which the enemy were firing at intervals. There an officer carried the children and they all ran as fast as they could, but Mrs. Inglis did not feel in the least afraid. In a large garden in the outskirts of the town they found the other women and children, and the officers of Sir Colin Campbell's force, who were all most kind, and feasted them with tea and bread and butter, which were great luxuries. Sir Colin came and talked to Mrs. Inglis for some time and was most attentive, but she said that all the while she knew that he was wishing them very far away, and no wonder, for without the women and children to take care of, he would have been free to attack the enemy. It was ten at night before they started on their journey with an escort of soldiers. Mrs. Inglis with her three children and three other ladies and another child were squeezed tightly together in one bullock waggon. She had only just got her baby to sleep when the word halt was called, silence was ordered, and all lights were put out. Clearly an attack was feared, and she was terrified lest her baby should begin crying again and betray where they were. After waiting in absolute silence for a quarter of an hour, the order was given to move on, and in two hours they reached a camp where tents had been got ready for them and food prepared and they could lie down and sleep. Next morning some of the officers invited Mrs. Inglis and her friends to breakfast, and she writes that, though she hopes she was not very greedy, she much appreciated the good things with which their table was loaded. The next day she had the great joy of receiving the home letters from her mother and friends in England which had been accumulating for five months, and she was able to write home herself.

Colonel Inglis had been left behind to bring out the garrison, which he did at night without the loss of any men. It was an immense relief to Mrs. Inglis when he reached the camp in safety. The next day they started on their march, the great procession of carriages and carts with the women, children, and luggage, guarded by the soldiers. They could only move very slowly and often had to stop because the carriages and carts got hemmed together. Several days were spent in this way. Mrs. Inglis could not see her husband every day, and great was her joy when he could visit her for a few minutes. She tells how on Sundays, if he came, they read the service together, and how at another time she could have a quiet walk and talk with him. They passed through Cawnpore, where a bright moon shone on the ruined houses, and everything reminded them of the horrors that had taken place there a few months before, when their fellow-countrywomen with their children had been cruelly butchered by the rebels. Eighteen days after leaving Lucknow they reached the railway. It had been a most trying and fatiguing journey, especially for the sick and wounded, over rough roads, in crowded, jolting carts. The train took them to Allahabad, where they were received with enthusiastic cheering from the crowds gathered to greet them, a reception which Mrs. Inglis felt most overpowering. At last they were in a safe place and could rest. By degrees steamers carried them down the Ganges to Calcutta. Mrs. Inglis was glad to linger amongst the last, for her husband was at Cawnpore with the troops, and at

Allahabad she could hear daily from him. She begged him to let her stay where she was, instead of going back to England, but he would not consent. As she travelled down the Ganges to Calcutta, a wearisome journey of three weeks in an overcrowded steamer, she heard from her fellow-passengers the stories of their hardships and losses. It was wonderful to think that she and her husband and three children were all safe. Strangely enough their dangers were not over yet, for the steamer that was taking them from Calcutta to England struck a rock and the passengers had to make their escape in small boats through the heavy surf. The waves were very high, and seemed as if they would swamp them, but little Johnny laughed merrily each time they broke over the boat. Fortunately they were picked up by a passing ship, and ultimately reached England in safety. Colonel Inglis stayed for some months in Cawnpore, but then his health broke down, which was not surprising after the terrible time he had been through. He was forced to ask for leave and was able to join his wife in England.

CHAPTER IX

Florence Nightingale

... ✦ ...

Florence Nightingale
(1820–1910)

Nurse,
reformer, and
symbol of mercy.

She brought
light to the
darkest wards
and changed
the heart of medicine.

Florence Nightingale, who has done so much to improve the nursing of the sick, was born on May 12, 1820, at Florence, in Italy, and was named after her birthplace. Her parents soon went back to live in England, where her father owned a country-house, called Lea Hurst, in Derbyshire. They spent their summers in Derbyshire, and in the autumn moved to Embley Park, in Hampshire, another house belonging to Mr. Nightingale. Florence grew up loving the country and the country people who lived round her home. As a little girl she was very fond of dolls, and used to pretend that they were ill, and nurse them, and bandage their broken limbs, with the greatest care and skill. She was devoted to animals and had many pets for whom she cared tenderly. Once, when she was out riding on her pony, she came upon an old shepherd whose dog had had his leg hurt by some mischievous boys. The shepherd thought that there was nothing to be done but to kill the dog to put it out of its misery. But Florence begged to be allowed to try to cure it. The leg proved not to be broken, and Florence poulticed it so cleverly that the dog was soon well again.

Florence was educated at home. Her father was very particular about her studies, and she learnt well and quickly. Even as a child she loved to visit sick people, and as soon as she was grown up, she spent most of her time in the cottages and in the village school. The old and the sick loved her visits, and her gentle, clever ways did much to ease their suffering. For the children, she invented all kinds of amusements, and delighted in playing with them. She also held a Bible class for the elder girls. So far her life had been spent much like that of many other English girls. She was pretty and charming and known to be very clever; she had travelled a good deal, and her home-life, with parents who delighted in her and one sister to whom she was devoted, was absolutely happy. But every year her interest in nursing the sick grew stronger. She had been much impressed by meeting Elizabeth Fry, and by hearing from her of the Institute of Kaiserswerth in Germany, where deaconesses were trained for nursing the sick poor. In order to find out how the sick were nursed in her own country, she visited some of the chief hospitals, and was grieved to find what ignorant, rough women the nurses were. They had no training, and did little for the comfort of the patients; the hospitals were dirty and badly kept, and the nurses were much given to drinking. Miss Nightingale also travelled in France, Germany, and Italy to visit the hospitals. There she found things on the whole much better, as the nursing was mostly done by nuns, or Sisters of Charity, religious women who had given their lives for the service of their fellow-creatures.

When she was twenty-nine, Miss Nightingale decided to go herself to Kaiserswerth to study nursing. She spent only a few months there, but she was delighted with what she saw and learned. Many years afterwards she wrote: "Never have I met with a higher love, a purer devotion than there. There was no neglect. The food was poor— no coffee but bean coffee—no luxury but cleanliness." She was much loved at Kaiserswerth; and an English lady who was there eleven years afterwards was told that many of "the sick remembered much of her teaching, and some died happily, blessing her for having led them to Jesus." Miss Nightingale wrote a little book about Kaiserswerth, in which she urged that women should be encouraged to work, and should be trained properly for their work. She herself at first used the knowledge that she had gained in tending the poor who lived near her own home. After a while, she moved to London that she might be able to help in other charitable work. She was interested in a Home that had been started for sick governesses, which she heard was in a very unsatisfactory condition, and went to live there herself, shutting herself off from all society that she might care for the sick women in the Home, and arrange for its proper management.

She was not at all strong, and after a time grew ill from the strain of too much work and had to go back to the country to rest.

It was about this time that England and France declared war on Russia, and the Crimean War began. England had not been at war for forty years, and the army was in no way well prepared. The country rejoiced to hear of the victory of the Alma won over the Russians, but people learnt with indignation of the sufferings of the soldiers after the battle. Nothing was ready for the care of the wounded, even food and clothing were scarce. Letters from the Crimea told terrible stories of the sufferings of the men. The French had fifty Sisters of Mercy to tend their sick, but the English had no female nurses. In the Times newspaper, a long letter, giving an account of the terrible state of things, was published, which ended with these words: "Are there no devoted women amongst us, able and willing to go forth to minister to the sick and suffering soldiers of the East in the hospitals at Scutari? Are none of the daughters of England, at this extreme hour of need, ready for such a work of mercy?" Many were stirred by this appeal and sent in offers of help to the War Office. Mr. Sidney Herbert, the Minister for War, was eager to send the needed help, but he felt that to send out women not trained for such work would be useless. He knew Miss Nightingale intimately, and it seemed to him that she was the one woman in England whose character and training fitted her to take the lead in this matter. He got the permission of the government to ask her to undertake the post of Superintendent of Nurses for the Crimea. Then he wrote to her to tell her the state of affairs. A large barrack hospital had been set apart for the sick and wounded soldiers at Scutari on the Bosphorus. Here the wounded were brought by ship from the Crimea. Masses of stores were being sent out, but there were no female nurses, and as women had never been employed to nurse soldiers, there were no experienced nurses ready to go, though many devoted women had offered their services. Mr. Herbert felt that there would be great difficulty in ruling the band of untrained nurses, and in making the new arrangements work smoothly with the medical and military authorities. He told Miss Nightingale that, if she would go, she should have full authority over the nurses, and the support of the government in all she might wish to do. He said that the whole success of the plan depended upon her willingness to go, and that her experience, her knowledge, her place in society gave her the power to do this work which no one else possessed. In those days it was quite a new thing to think of a lady being a nurse at all, and quite an unheard-of thing that a lady should go to nurse soldiers. Mr. Herbert thought that if this new plan succeeded, it would do an enormous amount of good both then and afterwards.

Miss Nightingale too, had read the letter in the Times , and was thinking over it in her home in the country. Before Mr. Herbert's letter reached her, she wrote to him of her own accord offering her services to go as nurse to the hospitals at Scutari. The moment had come for which unconsciously she had been long preparing, and she was ready for the work which came to her. Her letter crossed Mr. Herbert's. It was written on October 15, 1854, and immediately it was announced in the Times that Miss Nightingale had been appointed Superintendent of Nurses at Scutari. She at once set to work to collect the band of thirty-eight nurses whom she was to take out with her. There were a few Institutions in existence for training nurses, and to these Miss Nightingale appealed for volunteers. Twenty-four of those she took out came from such places. Six days after she had made her offer to go, she was ready to start with her band complete. They crossed the Channel to Boulogne, where the people had heard of their coming; the fishwives turned out to meet them, and insisted on carrying their bags from the boat to the train. They, too, were interested in the war where English and French soldiers were fighting side by side, and as they walked with them they begged the nurses to take care of any of their dear ones should they meet them. With tears and warm shakes of the hand they bade farewell to them, crying, "Long live the sisters," as the train carried them away.

On November 4th, Miss Nightingale and her nurses reached Scutari, where the poor men in hospital had heard of their coming, but could not believe the good news. One man cried when he saw them, exclaiming, "I can't help it when I see them. Only think of English women coming out here to nurse us! It seems so homelike and comfortable." It was a terrible state of things that Miss Nightingale found in the hospitals. The filth, misery, and disorder were indescribable. In the long corridors the wounded men lay crowded together; many of them had not even had their wounds dressed, nor their broken limbs set. There were no vessels for water, no towels or soap, no hospital clothes. The men lay in their uniforms, stiff with blood. The beds were reeking with infection, and rats and vermin of every kind swarmed over them. There was no time to plan reforms or to bring any order into the hospitals before more wounded from the battle of Inkermann arrived in terrible numbers, only twenty-four hours after Miss Nightingale had come. Her courage rose to the occasion, terrible though it was, and inspired her companions.

Whilst they all worked without ceasing to do what they could to help the worst suffering, she, in the midst of all her labours, thought out what could be done to bring order into the awful confusion. She had to see that proper supplies of all the things needed for the comfort of the soldiers were sent out from England, and to make arrangements for the distribution of the stores when they arrived. Her energy and her disregard of some of the rules laid down by the military authorities about the distribution of the stores made some people very angry, and there was a good deal of grumbling at what they considered her unnecessary haste and her interference. But Miss Nightingale cared for nothing so long as she could do the task for which she had been sent out. She set up a kitchen where food could be cooked for the sick and wounded, and a laundry where their clothes could be washed and disinfected. She wrote to England clear accounts of the state of things she had found, without any grumbling, but pointed out what had to be done for the proper care of the men. Opposition to her ways disappeared as it became clear how admirable were the results of her work. She won the orderlies to work with the utmost patience and devotion under the direction of the lady nurses; so that she could say that not one of them failed her in obedience, thoughtful attention, and considerate delicacy. They were rough, ignorant men, but in the midst of scenes of loathsome disease and death they showed to Miss Nightingale and her nurses the most courteous chivalry and constant gentleness, and she never heard from them a word that could shock her.

Florence Nightingale at Scutari—A Mission of Mercy.
(After the Picture by Jerry Barrett.)

The gratitude and devotion of the patients to her knew no bounds. At nights she used to pass through the long corridors, and the endless wards—there were four miles of wards in the hospital—carrying a little lamp in her hand, so as to see that all was well, and from this the patients learnt to call her "the lady of the lamp." They felt that she was their good angel, and one of them said afterwards, describing the comfort it was even to see her pass, "She would speak to one and another, and nod and smile to many more, but she could not do it to all for we lay there by hundreds; but we would kiss her shadow as it fell, and lay our heads on the pillow again content."

Huddled together in two or three damp rooms in the basement of the hospital, Miss Nightingale found a great number of poor women, the wives of the soldiers, with their babies, living in the utmost misery and discomfort. She did not rest till she had arranged better quarters for them. Some ladies were found to befriend them. Those whose husbands had been killed in the war were sent back to England, many were given work in the laundry which Miss Nightingale had started, and a school was opened for the children.

Florence Nightingale in one of the Wards of the Hospital at Scutari.

When the winter came on, the sufferings of the soldiers increased. The army was engaged in the siege of Sevastopol, and Miss Nightingale described the sufferings endured by the soldiers there in a letter to a friend: "Fancy working five nights out of seven in the trenches! Fancy being thirty-six hours in them at a stretch, with no food but raw salt pork sprinkled with sugar, rum, and biscuit; nothing hot ... fancy through all this the army preserving their courage and patience as they have done. There is something sublime in the spectacle." The hospitals were crowded with men brought in ill from the results of this exposure. Early in 1855 fifty more trained nurses were sent out from England, and they came in time to help in a terrible outbreak of cholera which filled the hospital with new patients, most of whom died after a few hours' suffering. Frost-bitten men were brought in too from Sevastopol, and of all these sufferers at least half died in spite of the care of the nurses. Again and again it was Miss Nightingale who comforted the dying and received from them the last message to be sent to the dear ones at home. She wrote down their words and took care of their watches or other possessions which they wished to send home.

The hearts of people in England were stirred by all they heard of the sufferings of the soldiers and of the devotion of the nurses. Supplies of every kind were sent out in great quantities, and all that was needed was that their use should be wisely organised. Miss Nightingale was much helped by the arrival of M. Soyer, the famous French cook, who came out at his own expense to organise the cooking in the hospitals. He introduced new stoves and many reforms in the kitchens, and was a most devoted admirer of the Lady-in-Chief, as Miss Nightingale was called.

After six months' work at Scutari, Miss Nightingale set out to visit the hospitals in the Crimea itself. M. Soyer and several of her nurses went with her. She rode to the camp near Balaclava, where she could hear the thunder of the guns which besieged Sevastopol. As she passed through the camp, some of the men who had been her patients at Scutari recognised her, and greeted her with a hearty cheer. The hundreds of sick in the field hospital were delighted to receive a visit from the lady of whom they had heard so much. Afterwards she rode right up into the trenches outside Sevastopol, so that the sentry was alarmed at her daring. Next day she visited another hospital at Balaclava and left some of her nurses to work there. She was on board the ship which was to take her back to Scutari, when she was suddenly seized with a very bad attack of Crimean fever. The doctors said that she must at once be taken to the Sanatorium at

Balaclava. Laid on a stretcher she was carried by the soldiers up the mountain side. For a few days it was thought that she was dying, but presently the joyful news was spread that she was better. She herself says that the first thing that helped her to recover was her joy over a bunch of wild flowers that had been brought her. Whilst she lay ill she was visited by Lord Raglan, the Commander-in-Chief of the army, who wished to thank her for all that she had done for the troops. She would not hear of going back to England after her illness as her friends wished, but as soon as possible returned to Scutari.

In the autumn, Sevastopol fell, and this brought the war to an end. But Miss Nightingale would not return home as the hospitals were still full of sick and wounded who could not be moved. She paid another visit to the hospitals in the Crimea, and travelled from one place to another over the bad mountain roads, in a carriage which had been specially made for her. She did much for the comfort of the soldiers, who had to stay on in the Crimea, and started libraries for them and reading-huts where they could go to sit and read; lectures and classes were also provided for them, and arrangements made to enable them to send home easily money and letters to their families.

Before she left the Crimea, Miss Nightingale set up, at her own cost, a white marble cross twenty feet high as a monument to the dead. It was dedicated to the memory of the soldiers who had perished and to the nurses who had died in tending them, and on it was written in English and Russian, "Lord, have mercy upon us."

From all sides she received tributes for her services. The Sultan gave her a diamond bracelet; Queen Victoria sent her a beautiful jewel specially designed by Prince Albert. Speaking in the House of Lords, Lord Ellesmere said: "The hospitals are empty. The angel of mercy still lingers to the last on the scene of her labours; but her mission is all but accomplished. Those long arcades of Scutari, in which dying men sat up to catch the sound of her footstep or the flutter of her dress, and fell back on the pillows content to have seen her shadow as it passed, are now comparatively deserted. She may be thinking how to escape, as best she may, on her return, the demonstration of a nation's appreciation of the deeds and motives of Florence Nightingale." This was just what Miss Nightingale wished to do. The government offered to bring her home in a man-of-war, but she travelled quietly back under the name of Miss Smith, so that her uncommon name might not attract attention to her. When she got to her own home, she went in by the back door. Crowds of people used to gather round the park in the following weeks in the hope of seeing her, but she refused to receive any sort of public welcome.

As soon as the war came to an end, before Miss Nightingale had returned home, a movement was started to give her a testimonial from the nation. Her friends had said that the only testimonial she would accept would be one which would help on the cause of providing trained nurses for the hospitals; and a Nightingale Hospital Fund was started to be given to her on her return to start her work of reform. Public meetings were held in support of this fund and when Miss Nightingale got back it had reached £48,000. With the help of friends she considered how best this money could be used. She was too ill to undertake herself as she had intended to manage the new institute for training nurses or to do more than advise from her sick room what had best be done. She had hoped that rest would completely restore her health, and even wished to go out to India to nurse when the mutiny broke out in 1857; but this was impossible. After her return from the Crimea she led almost continuously an invalid life; but it was not an idle life. She directed all the arrangements for using the Nightingale Fund, which was chiefly devoted to starting a school for training nurses at St. Thomas' Hospital in London; the Nightingale nurses will always keep alive the memory of her name. In all other matters connected with nursing she always took an active interest, especially in the health of the soldiers and in nursing in the army, and also in starting district nurses to nurse the sick poor in their own homes. Her advice was constantly sought, and she wrote many papers about nursing which were most useful, especially a very popular little book called "Notes on Nursing." But for more than fifty years since her wonderful work in the Crimea, she has lived a secluded life as an invalid, though it has been a life full of work and thought for the service of others. She is still living (in 1909) but is a complete invalid. The great lesson of her life is, that she had prepared herself so well that when the opportunity for doing a great piece of work came to her, she was able to use it. She had learnt and studied, and when the need came she was ready.

CHAPTER X

Isabella Bird, Afterwards Mrs. Bishop

··· ✧ ···

Isabella
Bird
(1831–1904)

Explorer,
writer, and
pioneer of
travel.

*She crossed
mountains
and cultures
with courage*
and an open
heart.

Isabella Bird, who afterwards became famous as a traveller, was the daughter of a clergyman. She was born in 1831, and spent her childhood in a country village in Cheshire of which her father was vicar. She was a frail, delicate child, and as it was good for her to be as much in the open air as possible, her father used to put her on a cushion before him when he rode round his parish. As soon as she was old enough, she rode a horse of her own, going with her father wherever he went. He made her notice everything they passed by the way, and questioned her about all that she saw. In after years she looked back to these early days as having taught her to be perfectly at home on a horse, to observe accurately everything that she saw, to love the flowers and the plants and to know their names and uses, to measure distances with her eye, and to watch the signs of the seasons. She was educated by her mother, and said that no one could teach as her mother did, since she made everything so wonderfully interesting. By the time she was seven, Isabella was an eager reader of books of all kinds, even of serious history. When she was eleven, her father moved to a parish in Birmingham, and there she soon became a keen Sunday school teacher and worker in the parish; later, her father again had a country living in Huntingdonshire. Isabella was not strong, and the doctor recommended a sea-voyage; so when she was twenty-three, she made her first journey, going to Canada and America. She wrote such interesting letters home describing all that she saw that her father urged her to make a book out of them, and soon after she came home her first book, "The Englishwoman in America" appeared, and it was much praised.

It was a bitter grief to Isabella when her father died in 1858. She spoke of him as the mainspring and object of her life. Her mother now settled in Edinburgh, and Isabella paid frequent visits to the Highlands and the Hebrides, and interested herself much in the condition of the Highlanders, who were then very poor. She helped many to emigrate, and worked hard to provide outfits for them. She was often ill, but wrote a great deal whilst lying on her sofa; she brought out another book about America, and sent many articles to magazines. Writing was very easy to her. After some years in Edinburgh, Mrs. Bird died, a crushing sorrow to her two daughters. Isabella wrote: "She has been my one object for the eight years of her widowhood." Isabella sought comfort in working for the poor people in Edinburgh and tried to do something to get rid of the miserable slums in that city. She wrote a book about them to rouse people to a sense of shame. Her hard work was often interrupted by distressing illness; she suffered a great deal from her spine, but even when ill, she managed to read and study. The doctors recommended a voyage for her health, and parting with much sorrow from her sister, she started in 1872 for New York and went on from there to New Zealand and then to the Sandwich Islands. She loved the sea and wrote that it was like living in a new world, it was so free, so fresh, so careless, so unfettered. The beauty of the Sandwich Islands fascinated her, and the book she wrote about her visit to them helped others to enjoy what she had seen.

She went next to America, determined to explore the Rocky Mountains, which were then much less known than they are now. Her journey amongst the mountains was made on horseback; her habit of riding since her childhood and her intimate knowledge of horses enabled her to spend with real enjoyment long days riding through the mountains, on steep and difficult paths, and sometimes in wild snowstorms. She rode astride like a man, in a dress which she had devised for herself, consisting of full Turkish trousers with frills reaching to her boots, over them a skirt which came down to her ankles, and a loose jacket. She stayed in log huts with settlers in the mountains, helping them with their work and much interested in watching the kind of life they led. The scenery was magnificent, and the fine air and the free open life suited her, and made her feel well and strong. She spent some time with some settlers in a high valley amongst the mountains, sleeping alone in a log hut. She used to ride out with the men to help them drive in the cattle which had strayed on the mountains, and managed so well that they called her a good cattle-man. Towards the end of October she started on a long ride through the mountains alone. She had luggage for some weeks, including a black silk dress packed behind her saddle, and felt very independent. The greater part of her journey was through a white world, for the mountains were covered with snow and the nights were intensely cold. The nights she passed generally in log huts with the settlers, who were always glad to show her hospitality. Some of the men were very wild and rough, but they always behaved well to her, and she came to trust and admire many of the men of the mountains and loved to hear their talk about the wonderful world of nature in which they lived. The newspapers wrote about the strange English woman and her lonely ride through the mountains, and often when she reached a new place, she found that the people had already heard of her.

One man she came across, who was known as Mountain Jim, was leading a very wild life, but had been a gentleman of good birth and education. Meeting her and riding about with her brought out all that was good in him. He gave up his evil habits of drinking, swearing, and fighting, and became a changed man. He was bitterly grieved at parting from her, but promised to keep straight, and his letters to her showed that he did. Unfortunately, not many months afterwards, he was shot by another man in a fit of passion.

Miss Bird got back to her sister in Edinburgh after nearly two years' travelling, and set to work to make a book out of her letters home. She could never stay quiet for long and travelled about in England, Scotland, and Switzerland, and when in Edinburgh was busy with all kinds of work for others. Soon she began to dream of another long journey. This time it was Japan she wished to visit; she dreaded parting from her sister, but she was always better travelling than when at home, and hoped that another journey would still more improve her health. She started for Japan in 1878, when she was forty-seven years old, determined not to go to the well-known places but to the almost unknown interior of the country. She was told that the difficulties in the way of such a journey would be very great, and that no English lady had as yet travelled through the interior. When she reached Japan many tried to dissuade her from her plans, but she engaged a Japanese servant and made her preparations for her journey, in spite of feeling a little nervous. She was afraid of being afraid. But very soon she could laugh at her fears and misfortunes, though she had endless discomforts to put up with. Everywhere there were fleas and mosquitoes, and as strangers were seldom seen in the interior, she was tormented by the crowds who turned out to see her and allowed her no privacy. Still she found that the Japanese crowds were quiet and gentle and did not press rudely upon her. As she got further inland, the villages became horribly dirty, and the women were filthy and hardly clothed. Her servant was deeply grieved that she should see such things, and once sat on a stone with his face buried in his hands, he was so distressed.

Her journey was made fatiguing by bad horses, and by very bad weather. Rain fell in torrents, and she was glad to use one of the straw rain cloaks which the Japanese women wear. But she was not discouraged by the difficulties of her first journey, and determined to visit Yezo, the island north of Japan, where live a wild people known as the hairy Ainos. In order really to study the ways of these people, she spent three days and two nights in the hut of their chief, sleeping in a sort of bunk in the wall, with a mat hung in front of her. The men of the place used this hut as a club, and crowded in at night to sit round the fire piled up with logs. She wrote: "I never saw such a magnificent sight as that group of magnificent savages with the fitful firelight on their faces, and the row of savage women in the background." They were very kind and courteous to her; she was treated as an honoured guest in every house she entered, and she returned their kindness by attending to the sick. It was with real regret that she left the friendly, gentle Ainos, after carefully studying their habits and manner of life. She returned to Tokio, the capital of Japan, and stayed two months with the British minister, studying Japanese ways and making excursions into the neighbourhood. From there she sailed to Hong-Kong and then to Canton and the Malay States, and then turned homewards, stopping at Cairo on the way, where she fell very ill. Her travels in the East had not suited her health, but they had filled her with new interests and taught her many things. Her books about her travels were better written after this, and attracted much admiration and interest. She was becoming a famous woman. But all the enjoyment of her success was spoilt to her by the serious illness of her beloved sister, who died the year after Miss Bird's return.

Miss Bird was now alone in the world, but she had a devoted friend in Dr. Bishop, who had for some years attended her sister and was with her in her last illness. He had several times asked Miss Bird to marry him, but she had always said that her heart was given to her sister. Now in her loneliness, he repeated his request and she at last consented, and they were married in the spring after her sister's death. She was fifty, ten years older than her husband. He promised that when the need of travel awoke in her, she should go to whatever end of the earth beckoned to her. He used to say that the only rival he had in her heart was the high tableland of Central Asia. As it turned out she never left him for long. He became ill soon after their marriage, and was almost a complete invalid till he died five years afterwards. Dr. Bishop was a man of noble character, and Mrs. Bishop was devoted to him and mourned him all her life. She was now altogether alone except for her friends, and there was no one to keep her from the long and dangerous journeys in wild countries which she loved. She, who was always ill when in civilised countries, often spending weeks on her sofa because of pains in her back, seemed to be able to endure anything when she was travelling and leading a wild, free life. One thing that helped her was that she was able to eat anything. Dr. Bishop said that she had the appetite of a tiger and the digestion of an ostrich. At first after her husband's death, she busied herself with bringing out her books of travel and with caring for the poor people amongst whom her sister had worked. She also wished to learn nursing, and spent three months in London in the surgical wards of a hospital. Dr. Bishop had been much interested in medical missions, and she decided to found a mission hospital in his memory. It was nearly three years after his death when she started on her next long journey, going first to India and on to Kashmere, where she thought of founding her hospital.

In her early days Mrs. Bishop had felt no interest in missions, indeed she rather disliked them. She thought it a mistake to interfere with the ways and beliefs of other people, and on her travels used to try to avoid mission houses. Dr. Bishop's influence had changed her opinion by first giving her an interest in medical missions; what she saw afterwards in Eastern countries turned her into a warm friend of all Christian missions. She made great friends with Dr. Neve, the medical missionary of the Church Missionary Society in Kashmere, and with him arranged for the building of the John Bishop Memorial Hospital at Islamabad. It was a great pleasure to her that Dr. Neve had been a student under her husband. When this was settled, she was glad to escape from the crowds of Anglo-Indians who haunted Kashmere, and whose hubbub she found intolerable, for a ride of twenty-eight days through the Himalayas to Lesser Thibet as far as Leh, travelling alone with native servants and camping out at night. When she got back to India, she found it possible to carry out a long cherished plan and make a journey into Persia. Before she started, she visited several mission stations, and founded another hospital in memory of her sister, called the Henrietta Bird Hospital, which also was under the care of an old pupil of her husband's.

The journey through Persia began at Bagdad and lasted nearly a year. The first part lay through wild lonely mountains, where no English lady had ever been; here she had the companionship of an English officer, who was travelling for scientific purposes. It was an awful journey, and she would never have undertaken it had she known the hardships she would have to face—the long marches, the wretched food, the abominable accommodation, the brutal barbarism of the people. The weather was terrible: ceaseless rain, or deep snow in the high mountains. The nights had to be spent in cold, filthy caravanserais, as the rough inns of the East are called, mere shelters, which three or four hundred mules and their drivers often shared with Mrs. Bishop's party. There was constant danger from robbers, and everywhere curious crowds surrounded her, allowing her no rest or peace; they used to feel and pull her hair, to finger all her things, and examine her clothes when she hung them up at night. They brought their sick in crowds to her to be healed. One evening, when she had got a mud hovel to herself and was suffering from a severe chill, lying down covered with blankets, she heard a noise, and looking up saw the room thronged with men, women, and children, covered with sores, and suffering from all kinds of diseases. She had to get up and listen for two hours to their tales of suffering, interpreted to her by her servant. It was painful indeed to be able to do but little for them. The next morning they were all there again. She could only give them ointments for their sores, lotions for their eyes, or some few simple medicines, and had to send most of them sadly away. The cold was so bitter and the storms so terrible in crossing the mountains that it was a wonder that Mrs. Bishop and her whole party did not perish. She felt that they would never have got through had it not been for the splendid Arab horses which carried them with unfailing spirit through all the difficult places.

Forty-six days brought them to Teheran, one of the chief cities of Persia, and here she rested in comfort for three weeks in the house of the English minister, and then they started for another and longer journey of exploration among the mountains. Again terrible hardships and dangers were endured. Every day after the fatigues of the journey, diseased and infirm people crowded her camp, and she did all she could to help them. One of the chiefs came to her one day for medicine, and as he lingered, watching her care for the people, he asked her why she took so much trouble for people unknown to her. She answered by telling him, through her interpreter, the story of Jesus Christ. When he had heard what she had to say, he said sadly, "He is the Hakim (doctor) for us, send us such a one as He was."

These people are Mahometans, and seeing the little help and comfort their religion gave to them, and the miserable lives to which it condemned their women, made Mrs. Bishop still more keen about Christian missions. In the larger towns she often visited the houses of the chiefs, and went into the women's quarters, where the many wives of the chief and his children lived shut up together. They were never allowed to go out, and spent their days in quarrelling, eating sweetmeats, and dressing and dyeing their hair. They asked her for love potions and charms, and wondered why she did not dye her hair, and for what purpose she could be travelling.

For the last part of her journey, Mrs. Bishop was quite alone with her servants, as the English officer had to go elsewhere. Her chief companion was the Arab horse on which she rode, which she called "Boy," and which was as gentle and affectionate as a child. He often slept in her tent, and would come and rub his nose against her face to attract her attention. He carried her safely from Burjurid, in the centre of Persia, to Trebizond, on the shores of the Black Sea, a journey of four months. In dangers and hardships her courage never failed. She was robbed of most of her travelling necessaries, and had to do without them as she could not replace them; she had strange food, and often had to do without food at all; and yet she got safely through though she was a small, delicate woman, fifty-nine years of age. In all she had travelled 2500 miles since she started on her journey through Persia. Wherever there were mission stations, she enjoyed the hospitality of the missionaries, and she was much impressed by their self-denying work. The last part of her journey was through Armenia where she saw with much sympathy the courage and endurance of the Christian Armenians, poor, ignorant people, who clung to their ancient faith in spite of cruel persecution. They begged her to send them teachers, for their own priests were poor and ignorant because they could not afford to go away to study. One of the priests said to her, "Beseech for a teacher to come and sit among us and lighten our darkness." England he thought could send teachers, for he said, "England is very rich."

From Trebizond Mrs. Bishop travelled quickly back to England, and was soon very busy preparing a book with an account of her travels. But she found time to speak at many missionary meetings, so anxious was she to plead the cause of the poor people whom she had seen. Her pleasant voice and way of speaking and all the interesting things she had to tell made people eager to hear her, and she spoke also to gatherings of learned men. She was considered one of the greatest of missionary advocates, and an address, in which she pleaded for the poor secluded women in Eastern lands, was printed and sent all over the world. She spoke of the terrible sins of the non-Christian lands in the East and of the degradation of the women, and said she would give all she had to help them.

As usual when at home Mrs. Bishop was constantly ill, and only three years passed before she started on another journey. She longed for the East and wished to visit China and Japan. Whilst she was at home, she had taken lessons in photographing, that she might be able to take better photographs on her travels. She improved immensely, and after this her books were always illustrated by her own beautiful photographs. She first went to Korea, the strange country which lies between China and Japan, and which both those countries desired to possess. At first she did not like Korea nor its people, but she soon grew to love them, and especially enjoyed the beautiful, sunny climate. She wrote that she felt this journey to be more absorbing in its interest than any she had yet had. During the three years that she now spent in the East, she paid three visits to Korea, in order that she might thoroughly study the land and its people. She had a great many hardships to go through in some parts of her journey. Once after riding for eleven hours under a hot sun, she found the only night's lodging she could get was in a filthy fishing village full of the vilest smells. Her room in the inn was such an awful black hole, full of vermin and rats, that when her Chinese servant left her for the night he said, "I hope you won't die." In other places she was annoyed by the crowds who came to stare at her, never having seen an Englishwoman before. Once her servant had his arm broken by a fall from his horse, and she was obliged to set it herself. He was so touched with her care of him that, in spite of his pain, he somehow managed to do his work just as usual, and said, "The foreign woman looked so sorry, and touched my arm as if I had been one of her own people. I shall do my best."

Between her visits to Korea, Mrs. Bishop went back to Japan, and also travelled in China. Her first object was to visit the mission stations in China, and she was much interested in all she saw, especially in the medical missions, and was full of admiration for the missionaries. On a second visit to China she made a long journey into the interior, going up first by boat on the river Yangtze for 300 miles, and then alone 300 more miles into the country in a carrying chair borne by Chinese, the only way of travelling. Far in the interior, she visited the missionaries of the China Inland Mission, and there she gave money to found a hospital to be called the Henrietta Bird Hospital after her sister. Wherever she went she photographed, undisturbed by the curious crowds who gathered round her. Once as she was being carried along, the people got so angry because she would not stop her chair to let them have a good look at her, that they threw stones at her, and one hit her a sharp blow on the head from which she suffered for a long time.

In 1897, after an absence of over three years, Mrs. Bishop came back to London. She had accomplished these long and tiring journeys at the age of sixty-six. She brought back with her a beautiful collection of photographs which she had taken, and materials for writing two books, one on Korea and one on her travels in China. She busied herself with writing her books, lecturing about her travels, and speaking at missionary meetings and doing all she could for the cause of missions. She tried to settle down in a house, and took first one in London and then one in the country, but never stayed anywhere long, and was as usual always ill as soon as she tried to live in a civilised country. So after a while she went off to Morocco, and there at the age of seventy she travelled through the wild parts of the country, riding astride on a superb horse and camping out at night. This was her last journey. After she got back to England she still lectured and spoke for missions, and studied photography. She began to plan another journey to China, but she fell ill in Edinburgh. For some months she was confined to bed, but still saw her friends, and was full of eager interest in everything that happened. She was not afraid to die, and waited peacefully for the end, saying that she was going home. She died in March 1904, at the age of seventy-one. Those who wish to know about her travels and the wonderful things she saw must read her many books, which are full of life and adventure and enable us to share her experiences and admire her pluck and energy.

CHAPTER XI

Sister Dora

··· ✦ ···

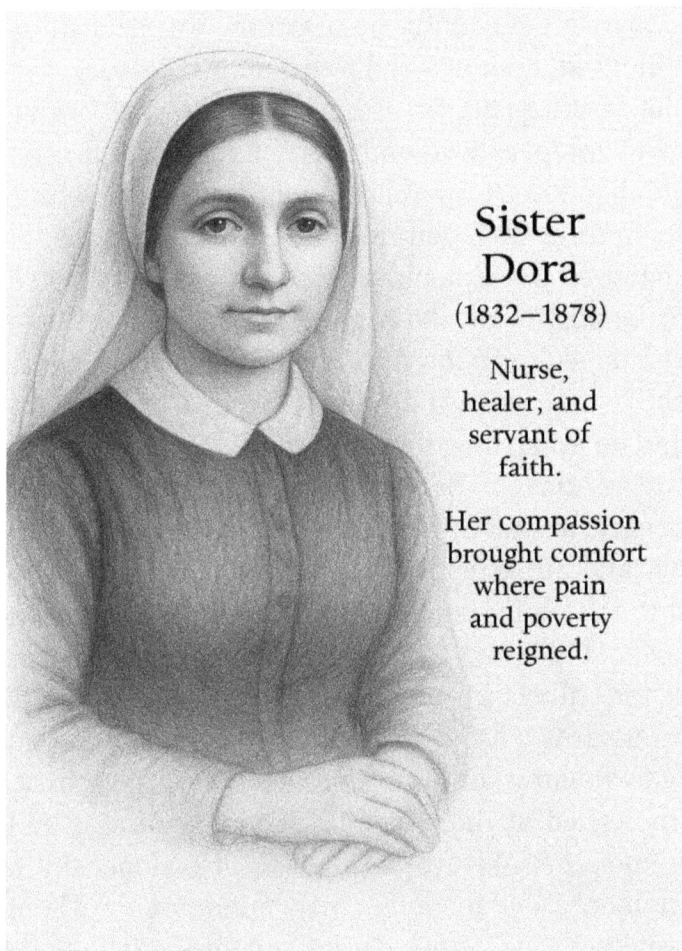

Sister
Dora
(1832—1878)

Nurse,
healer, and
servant of
faith.

Her compassion
brought comfort
where pain
and poverty
reigned.

Dorothy Pattison, who was afterwards known as Sister Dora, was born in 1832 in a little village called Hauxwell, near Richmond, in Yorkshire, of which her father was the rector. She was the youngest but one of a family of twelve children, of whom ten were daughters. They grew up in all the enjoyment of country life. Dorothy was delicate as a child and not allowed to do regular lessons, but she describes herself as having all the same been a great romp, as wild and merry as a boy, and good at all outdoor sports—riding, rowing, shooting, swimming, and skating. But even as a tiny child she loved to wash and nurse her dolls, and longed to be able to do the same for real people. When she talked over the future with her nearest sister she used to say, "I'll be a nurse or a lady doctor and do everything for my patients." When she was twelve, one of her sisters fell ill, and Dorothy begged, at first in vain, to be allowed to sit up with her and nurse her, but at last she managed to slip into the room unnoticed, and once she was there, she was allowed to stay and helped to nurse her sister till she was well. A couple of years afterwards a fever broke out in the village, and an old woman whom Dorothy knew very well took it. She called at the house to ask how she was and found the old woman left quite alone. In a moment, she made up her mind, and without thinking of what her parents might say, she hung up her coat and jacket behind the door and told the old woman she had come to stay with her. In the evening she sent a message home to say that she was going to stay all night, and word came back that, as she had chosen to stay without permission, she must now remain with the old woman. She washed her and nursed her and read the Bible to her, but she grew worse and worse, and the next night she died. A kind neighbour came in and helped to lay her out, but Dorothy, tired out and frightened, was left to spend the night alone in the cottage. Next morning she sent a message to the Rectory to say that the poor woman had died, might she come home. But the answer came back, "Stay where you are till you are sent for." She was terrified lest her parents had cast her off and she should never be allowed to go home. But soon a carriage arrived with her old nurse to carry her off to spend a month at the seaside, so that she might be free from all infection before going home. When at last she returned home she was welcomed as a little heroine, and got rather puffed up by the praise she received.

As she got stronger and able to study more, she was inclined to rebel at the time spent over lessons, and said she did not see why, as she was going to be a nurse, she should learn languages and music. But she was told that a nice Christian nurse should learn everything she had time for; she might some day have French or German patients, and music would be a pleasure to everybody; it would not do to be one-sided, for she ought to be able to care for the minds and souls of her patients as well as for their bodies. So she was persuaded to study gladly, and would often wonder how the thing she was learning would come in afterwards. Later she found that there was not a single thing she had learnt which had not in some way been hallowed in the service of God. She used to say to others, "Never feel that it is waste of time to get knowledge of any kind; you can never tell how handy it may come in."

Dora grew up to be a very handsome woman. By the time she was twenty, all her delicacy had disappeared and she was tall and strong. She had very high spirits and was always full of fun and ready to see the funny side of people and things. Her laughter and her happy voice, singing as she went about the house, were the delight of her father, who called her his sunshine. But though she loved her home and her rides and walks on the moors, she did not find there enough occupation for her active nature. Her mother died after a long time of ill-health, during which Dora had been one of her devoted nurses, and now Dora longed for some real work. Her father did not wish her to leave home, but he did not forbid it, and at last when she was twenty-nine, Dora went to be schoolmistress at Woolston, a little village in Buckinghamshire. She lived there alone in a tiny cottage, loving the children who came to her school, and making herself the friend of all the poor and sick in the village. She did not feel, however, that this was her real work; and after three years she decided to join the Sisterhood of the Good Samaritans. She had learnt to know these Sisters in Yorkshire, as they had their chief home at Coatham, which was not very far from her old home. The Sisters had a Convalescent Home under their care, and many of them went out from Coatham to work in other towns.

After she joined the Sisterhood, Sister Dora, as she was now called, had to work very hard. The Sisters did all the work of the house, and Sister Dora cleaned floors and grates, swept and dusted, and for a time acted as cook. She sometimes felt it very hard to have to do all this work. Once when a gentleman whom she knew came into the kitchen where she was peeling potatoes, she pulled her hood over her face so that he might not see her. In after life she found the great advantage of having learnt how to do all the work of a house herself. She thought some of the rules very strict; but still she was very happy there, and the Sisters loved her. She was able also to learn more about nursing, as the Sisters had a Cottage Hospital near Middlesborough, to which she was sent. Sometimes, too, she was sent to nurse private patients, and sometimes to nurse in another Cottage Hospital for accidents at Walsall, which was managed by the Coatham Sisters.

At last Sister Dora settled altogether at Walsall, in charge of the little hospital there. Walsall is a great manufacturing centre, with coal pits, blast furnaces, and many kinds of factories. It had then no large hospital; the little Cottage Hospital was chiefly intended for accidents, and the patients were for the most part men and boys from the pits and workshops. There were also a large number of out-patients, men, women, and children. As most of the cases were accidents, Sister Dora was particularly anxious to become a good surgical nurse, and the chief surgeon at the hospital, when he saw how quick and clever she was, taught her all that he could, so that she could attend to many cases herself without the help of the doctor. The hospital in which she at first nursed was very small and inconvenient, with only fourteen beds, but a few years after Sister Dora settled in Walsall a new hospital was built on the top of the hill on which the town lies. It had twenty-eight beds, conveniently arranged in three wards, so that it was just possible for an active woman like Sister Dora to do all the nursing herself. She had the help of an old servant of her family, who came to live with her and who soon learnt to be a very capable nurse herself. Other women were engaged to sit up at night with the patients, and, later, Sister Dora used to have lady pupils who learnt nursing under her.

It was a very hard life, full of ceaseless work and responsibility, but Sister Dora threw her whole heart into it, and loved her work and the people for whom she worked. Once settled at Walsall, she never wished to leave it. Speaking to a friend about her work, she said, "I generally find that the more I have to do the stronger and happier I feel. It is hard enough sometimes at night, when I have been round to all the patients and left them comfortable and asleep, and am just going to bed myself, to be called down by the bell, or perhaps roused by it just as I am falling asleep. But then I think 'the Master calleth thee,' and jump up and go down, to find perhaps some poor drunken man or woman, and it is difficult to recognise the Master in such poor degraded creatures as come to be doctored up." She had a wonderful power over the men and boys amongst whom she worked. She sympathised deeply with all their pain and trouble, and made them feel as if their troubles were her own, but she tried to make them forget their pain by her bright talk and her laughter and jokes. She would raise their spirits by her delightful fun, till an Irishman said once, "Make you laugh! she'd make you laugh when you were dying." Whenever she had a spare minute, she would read to them or talk to them or play games with them. She allowed no bad talk or quarrelling in the wards, and tried to mend her patients' morals as well as their limbs. They each of them knew that they had a real friend in her, and that she prayed for each and cared deeply what became of them. They loved to come and see her after they had left the hospital, and were always sure of a welcome. She tried hard to cure them from their drinking ways, showing them again and again how hard it was to heal the wounds of those who drank; and when they were brought in at night wounded after a drunken brawl, after dressing their wounds with all her usual gentleness, she would ask them why they did not behave like respectable members of society, instead of fighting in the streets and getting her up at unearthly hours of the night to mend their broken heads.

Sister Dora was devoted to children and they loved her, and she knew how to get them to bear patiently the dressing of their wounds. Often when a child was miserable and in pain, she would carry it about with her on one arm as she went through the wards, saying, "Don't you cry, Sister's got you," whilst with her other hand she attended to the patients. Many children suffering from terrible burns used to be brought to the hospital, and she grew so clever in treating them that the surgeons trusted them entirely to her care. Once a child was brought in so badly burnt that it was plain it had only a few hours to live. All pain had ceased, but the child was terrified. Sister Dora gave up all other work in order to comfort her. She sat by the bed for some hours talking to her about Jesus Christ and His love for little children, and about heaven where she would never feel hunger and pain again. The child grew peaceful and happy, and her last words were, "When you come to heaven, Sister, I'll meet you at the gates with a bunch of flowers."

Sister Dora felt special sympathy for the men who had been so hurt that it seemed necessary for them to have an arm or leg cut off. She knew well how difficult this made it for them to earn a livelihood, and she devoted all her skill to saving the wounded limb if possible. One night a fine healthy young man was brought in with his arm torn and twisted by a machine. The doctor said that nothing could save it, and that he must cut it off at once. Sister Dora was moved by the despair of the poor man; she looked long at his arm and at himself, and the man cried out, "O Sister! save my arm for me; it's my right arm." When she turned to the doctor and asked if she might try to save the arm, he only asked her if she was mad, and said that the man's life could not be saved unless his arm were taken off at once. But she turned to the patient and said, "Are you willing for me to try to save your arm, my man?" He was willing, but the surgeon was very angry, and refused to help her, saying, "Remember, it's your arm," and telling her she must take all the responsibility. Night and day for three weeks she tended him, naturally feeling terribly anxious as to what would happen. She often said afterwards, "How I prayed over that arm." At the end of that time she asked the surgeon to come and look at her work, and when she unbandaged the arm and showed it to him, straightened and in a healthy, promising condition, he exclaimed, "Why you have saved it, and it will be a useful arm to him for many a long year." It is not surprising that Sister Dora wept with joy at her success, nor that the man became one of her most devoted admirers. He was nicknamed "Sister's Arm" in the hospital, and used to come back often to see her after he had left.

Another man himself tells how she had to persuade him to allow his leg to be taken off as the only way of saving his life. He had grown so thin and wasted that she used to carry him upstairs in her arms so that he might join in the prayers she held for the whole hospital. He was eight months in the hospital, and he says, "I learned to love

Sister Dora as a mother." He tells how she used in the afternoons to attend to the out-patients, "dress their wounds, set a broken arm, sew up a cut, or draw teeth, in fact anything that was required of her she would do, and always with the tenderest care and the kindest word to all." She often amused the men with tales of her doings in the country as a girl, and told them about her riding and fox-hunting, and this man who watched her life in the hospital for eight months says, "those patients who were the most trouble, she seemed the fondest of." She knew how to get the men to help her by making them wait upon one another; generally there was some boy who had to stay a long while in the hospital, who waited upon her as a devoted slave. After she had been four years at the hospital, to show their gratitude for all she had done, her patients subscribed fifty pounds amongst themselves with which they bought a small carriage and pony for her. She delighted in using it to send convalescents for a drive, and found it a help in taking her to visit sick people in their homes. She seldom took a holiday herself, and once was three years at the hospital without any break, but if she did go away into the country with friends, she enjoyed everything with all her old energy, bathing or skating, taking long walks, when she would lead the way in scaling fences or fording streams. Sometimes she took patients who were convalescent for expeditions into the country or to visit Lichfield Cathedral. The old patients specially loved to revisit the hospital on Sundays, when, after a clergyman had held a short service, Sister Dora used to speak to them herself, and then lead them in the singing of many hymns. She always had a small Bible in her pocket, and studied it whenever she had a spare minute.

In 1875 there was a terrible outbreak of smallpox in Walsall. There was an isolation hospital on the outskirts of the town, but in those days people were not compelled by law to send smallpox patients away, and they refused to go of their own accord, for they said that they would rather die at home. It was very necessary for the welfare of the town that they should be persuaded to go to the hospital and not spread the terrible infection by staying in their own homes. So Sister Dora offered to leave her hospital and go to take charge of the Smallpox Hospital. She knew that the people trusted her, and thought that they would come if she was there. Her offer was gladly accepted; all through the town the news ran, "Sister is going to the Epidemic Hospital." Her lady pupils were left to take charge of the hospital, and she went off to her lonely work with the surgeon of the hospital to show her the way. It seemed such a lonely and desolate spot that even

226

her courage failed her at the door, and she cried out, "Oh take me back, I cannot endure this dreadful place." But the surgeon knew her real courage, and only said, "Come in." It was an admirably planned little hospital, and she was delighted with it. There were twenty-eight beds, and she had not been half-an-hour in the hospital before seven patients arrived, to be followed by many more. Her only regular helper was the porter, an old man, who did all he could for her when he was sober, but used sometimes to go away and get drunk, leaving her alone for the whole night. Two old women came in from the workhouse to help her in washing the clothes and bedding, but much of the scrubbing and cleaning she had to do herself, as well as all the nursing. One of the police who came to see her told her that the people in the town declared they should not mind having the smallpox with "Sister" to nurse them. Some few people were brave enough to visit her in her loneliness, and to bring her books and flowers and news of her patients at the hospital.

One of the old patients, an engine-stoker, went often to see her after his day's work was done. He had been twice in the hospital under her care, and he said, "I could not tell you all her goodness to me, words would fail me if I tried." She was full of courage and joy in her work, and wrote to a friend: "You must not fret. I rejoice that He has permitted one so unworthy to work for Him; and oh, if He should think me fit to lay down my life for Him, rejoice, rejoice, at so great a privilege." Even her sense of fun did not leave her, and she wrote a long letter to her old patients at the Cottage Hospital, calling them all by their nicknames and sending messages to each. She said of a boy who was her special slave: "What shall I say to my beloved Sam. I wish I had my boy here. I send him twenty kisses and hope he has been in church to-day and in time. He must not sulk all the time I am away. I have two blessed babies, who alternately keep up music all day and night, accompanied by an Irishwoman's tongue, so I am not dull. Have you been singing to-day? You must sing particularly, 'Safe in the arms of Jesus' and think of me. Living or dying, I am His. Oh, my children, you all love me for the very little I do for you; but oh, if you would only think what Jesus has done, and is doing for you, your hearts would soon be full of love for Him, and you would all choose Him for your Master."

Towards the middle of May, the Smallpox Hospital was empty and she hoped soon to leave; but before she was ready to go new patients were brought in, and this happened several times, so that it was not till the middle of August, after six months' work at the Smallpox Hospital, that she was able to close it.

The following October a terrible explosion occurred at the furnace of some ironworks, and eleven men were covered with streams of molten metal. In their agony they jumped into a neighbouring canal, and were with difficulty rescued and taken in cabs to the hospital. Burnt all over and frightfully disfigured, they were carried in and laid on the floor till a ward could be cleared for them. It was a terrible scene, even the doctors could hardly stay in the ward, but Sister Dora never ceased in her devoted care of the men. Cries came from most of them, "Sister, come and dress me." "Do dress me," "Oh, you don't know how bad I am." She could only answer, "Oh my poor men, I'll dress you all, if you'll give me time." One poor man, seeing how distracted she was by the different cries for help, said, "Sister Dora, I want to be dressed very bad, but if there's any wants you worse go and do them first." He was in terrible pain and died during the night. Of the eleven only two recovered. Some lingered for as long as ten days, and during that time Sister Dora never went to bed, and hardly left the ward. One of those who survived described how she went from bed to bed talking, laughing, even joking with the men; telling them stories, doing everything she could to distract them from their pain, and pointing out the way to heaven to those who were to die. He spoke with delight of her visits to his bedside at night when he was recovering, saying, "It did you good only to look at her," and ending with, "What we felt for her I couldn't tell you; my tongue won't say it."

One result of this terrible accident was that the ward in which the burnt men had lain was so poisoned that it could not be used again, and it was decided to build a new hospital. In the meanwhile, a house was fitted up as a temporary hospital. It was a tiring life for Sister Dora, as the temporary hospital was small and not at all convenient, and many patients had to be nursed in their own homes. It was at this time that she first began to find it difficult to lift her patients, and after a while she was compelled to consult a doctor about her health. He discovered that she had a mortal malady. It was possible that an operation might do her some good, but it was by no means certain. She determined to go on as usual, and made him promise to tell no one of her illness. She worked harder than ever and would not give in. She drove about in her little pony carriage to visit her patients, and no one was allowed to know that anything was wrong with her. Then an outbreak of fever in the temporary hospital made it necessary to close it, and as the new hospital was not yet ready it was possible for

Sister Dora to leave Walsall. She visited her relations and went to Paris and London to study improvements in surgical science. All the time her disease was growing worse, and still she told no one. Her wish was to die at Walsall amongst her own people, and as the hospital was not ready, a little house near to it was taken for her. People could not believe that she was dying. She was surrounded with all the care that love could give her, and often her visitors were surprised to see her, in spite of pain and weakness, still her old self, full of fun and jokes. Her interest in the new hospital was very keen, and she rejoiced that it was finished in time for her to know of its opening. She listened eagerly to all that was told her about it, and gave her advice about all the arrangements. Often she suffered terribly, and when at last she died, on Christmas eve, 1878, it was with relief that her friends heard that her pain was over. She was carried to her grave by some of the railway men for whom she had cared with so much devotion. The Bishop was there and great numbers of the clergy, and there came, too, hundreds of her patients and an immense crowd consisting of nearly all the people of the town.

The Statue at Walsall

When, later, it was discussed what memorial of her should be placed in Walsall some suggested a Convalescent Home, as what she herself would most have desired; but the working men of the town were quite clear that what they wanted was a statue of Sister Dora. One of them said that of course they could not forget her, but that they wanted her to be there, so that when strangers came and saw the statue and asked who it was, they might answer, "Who's that? Why that's our Sister Dora." So her statue in her nurse's dress, as she lived and worked amongst them, stands in the centre of Walsall to remind the people of her life of love. The workmen spoke of her as "the most saintly thing that was ever given us."

CHAPTER XII

Queen Victoria

··· ✦ ···

Queen Victoria
(1819–1901)

Monarch, mother, and emblem of an age.

Her reign united a nation and reshaped the modern world.

It is impossible in one short chapter to tell about all the things that made Queen Victoria's reign famous, and I am only going to tell something about her own life and to try to show what kind of a woman she was. Her father was the Duke of Kent, son of King George III., and her mother was a German princess. The Princess Victoria was their only child, and she was born in 1819 in Kensington Palace. It was possible that the little princess might some day be Queen of England, but at her birth she had three uncles living, older than her father, who would all have a right to the throne before her. She was only a few months old when her father and grandfather died and her eldest uncle became king as George IV. Her mother, a German lady, was very lonely in England. Her chief adviser was her brother Leopold, then living in England; he made the Duchess of Kent feel how important her position was as mother of the child who might be queen some day. He said that she must be brought up in England; so the duchess consented to live on at Kensington Palace and devoted herself to the education of her child. In after years the Queen, writing about her childhood, said that her chief pleasure was visiting her uncle Leopold, who lived at Claremont, near Esher. She was brought up very simply and always slept in her mother's bedroom. When she stayed at Claremont or by the seaside, where they often went, she did her lessons in her governess's bedroom. She was not fond of learning, and did not know her letters till she was five. George IV. had quarrelled with her father, and did not like her mother, and took very little notice of them; but she went as a child to see him at Windsor, and remembered how he took her by the hand, saying, "Give me your little paw." Next day he met her driving in the park and stopped his carriage and said, "Pop her in," and she was very pleased to drive by his side in the carriage with its servants in scarlet liveries.

When she was thirteen her mother gave her a small red morocco book in which to write her diary, and from that day till a few days before her death, she used to write down every night the events of the day. As a little girl she wrote down the hours of her lesson, when she went out riding, or was taken to the theatre or to hear music, and when she washed Dash, her pet dog.

The princess's governess was a German lady, Fräulein Lehzen, whom she adored, though she was greatly in awe of her; she spoke German before she learned English, but her mother took care that she should learn English well. When she was eight a clergyman, Mr. Davys, was appointed to direct her education. He chose a number of teachers for her, and himself taught her religion and history. Her life was strict and dull, and in after years she did not look back to her childhood as a happy time. George IV. died when she was six and was succeeded by his brother, William IV., who had no children, so that Princess Victoria was now heir to the throne. Her mother did not get on with William IV. and did not like her to go to court, and this made the King very angry, though he was always very kind to the little princess when she visited him privately. She was not allowed to go to his coronation, because the King and her mother could not agree as to the place she should take in the procession. This was a great disappointment and she wept bitterly—nothing could console her, not even her dolls.

Queen Victoria at her Accession. (Engraved by
Thompson after a Portrait by Lane.)

It was a great grief to the princess when her
uncle Leopold left England to become King of
Belgium. She was devotedly attached to him and

he to her, and she always looked to him for advice and guidance. They wrote to one another constantly in terms of the deepest affection. He recommended her books to read and discussed the affairs of Europe with her. As part of her education her mother used to take her on tours through different parts of England, when they visited the great nobles and some of the chief sights and most important cities. She was sometimes a little tired by all the stiff ceremonies she had to go through, though she liked seeing people. She was very fond of music and dancing, spent much of her time in singing, and learnt to play the harp.

Portrait of Prince Albert.

When she was sixteen, she was confirmed by the Archbishop of Canterbury, and he spoke to her so seriously about the duties of her position that she was drowned in tears and frightened to death. One of her uncle Leopold's most cherished plans was that the princess should marry her cousin, Prince Albert of Saxe-Coburg; and when she was seventeen, he arranged that Prince Albert, who was a few months younger, should visit England with his father and elder brother. The visit was a great success. The princess wrote to her uncle: "They are both very amiable, very good and kind, and extremely merry, just as young people should be. Albert is extremely handsome ... they are excessively fond of music, like me." A fortnight later she wrote: "I must thank you, my beloved uncle, for the prospect of great happiness you have contributed to give me in the person of dear Albert. Allow me, then, my dearest uncle, to tell you how delighted I am with him, and how much I like him in every way. He possesses every quality that could be desired to make me perfectly happy. He is so sensible, so kind, and so good, and so amiable too. He has, besides, the most pleasing and delightful exterior and appearance you can possibly see." Prince Albert thought his cousin very amiable and wonderfully self-possessed. Nothing was, however, said about marriage during this visit and the prince returned to Germany.

Just after the princess was eighteen, her uncle, King William IV., died, on June 20, 1837. She herself described in her journal what happened afterwards: "I was awoke at six o'clock by Mama, who told me that the Archbishop of Canterbury and Lord Conyngham were here and wished to see me. I got out of bed, and went into my sitting-room (only in my dressing-gown) and alone, and saw them." They told her that the King was dead, and, kneeling to kiss her hand, greeted as Queen the slim young girl just roused from sleep. A couple of hours later, Lord Melbourne, the Prime Minister, came to see her, and she wrote: "I saw him in my room and, of course, quite alone, as I shall always do all my ministers." She who had been so carefully guarded by mother and governess had now to act alone, and it seems, from the way she notes it in her journal, as if she was glad. She held her first Council that morning, and again writes that she went to it quite alone. There she read the speech that Lord Melbourne had prepared for her to the ministers and privy-councillors. Every one was struck with the way in which she bore herself. Though she was very short, not five feet tall, her movements were dignified and graceful. Her voice, which was very beautiful, was clear and untroubled and thrilled her hearers. The blush on her cheek added to the interest and charm of her appearance. Lord Wellington said, "She not merely filled her chair, she filled the room." She was quite composed; she wrote in after years that she took things as they came, as she knew they must be. What she was feeling she wrote that night in her diary: "Since it has pleased Providence to place me in this station, I shall do my utmost to fulfil my duty towards my country; I am very young, and perhaps in many, though not in all, things inexperienced, but I am sure that very few have more real good will and more real desire to do what is fit and right than I have;" she wrote, too, in large letters, "I AM QUEEN."

Viscount Melbourne.
From a figure in Hayter's Reformed Parliament in the
National Portrait Gallery.

She was delighted with the kindness of Lord Melbourne, her Prime Minister, and he from the first felt deeply the charm of the girl-queen, whose steps he guided like a father. After the quiet, dull life she had led hitherto, it was an amazing change for her, and she enjoyed it to the full. She loved meeting people and enjoyed the large dinners at which she presided. She loved her long rides with the ladies and gentlemen of her court; she enjoyed the court balls, at which she used to dance all night. But she was also determined from the first to do her work as Queen. She felt that the country was hers, that the ministers were hers, and that the people were her people, whom she had to govern. From the first she showed that as Queen she was going to be independent of her mother. The duchess lived with her but she had a separate set of rooms, and was allowed no share in public business. Long hours were spent by the Queen with Lord Melbourne, talking over public affairs, that she might learn to understand them. He constantly dined with her, and when he did always sat next her, and often talked to her of books and of people whom he had known. She wrote in her diary: "He has such stores of knowledge, such a wonderful memory; he knows about everybody and everything, and he imparts all his knowledge in such a kind and agreeable manner."

Another friend and adviser was Baron Stockmar, a German friend of the Queen's uncle, Leopold, whom he had sent to England to help her to understand politics. He was a wise man, of great knowledge, and taught the Queen how she must keep out of party politics, and what were the limits of her power. It was difficult to know exactly what was the power of the sovereign in England. The monarchy was not popular when Victoria became Queen. Neither George IV. nor William IV. had been much respected, and they had had little influence on affairs. Victoria had a high idea of her position as well as of her duties as Queen, but she had to learn exactly how much she was able to do. Sometimes she was deeply vexed when she could not get her own way, and she made some mistakes at first. But her strong sense of duty kept her in the right way, and showed her the kind of influence she could use. Her ministers might change, but she was always there, and as she took the greatest trouble to know all that was going on, and read all the most important dispatches written by her ministers, she soon got a very wide understanding of affairs, particularly of foreign politics. It was a strange life for a girl. All the morning she read dispatches, or signed her name to papers, or talked to her ministers. Then came her long rides, her music and singing, a game of battledore and shuttlecock with some of her ladies, a dinner, followed by dancing, music, cards, or wise talk with her ministers. She enjoyed it all, the power and the freedom, and the attention paid to her by the waiting crowds when she rode out.

Shortly after her accession, she went to live at Buckingham Palace. It had been built in the reign of George IV., but neither he nor William IV. had lived there; it was not at all a convenient house, and afterwards the Queen improved it very much. She at first thought Windsor a very melancholy place, but she learnt to like it when in the summer her uncle Leopold stayed there with her, and she wrote after his visit: "I have passed such a pleasant time here, the pleasantest summer I have ever passed in my life." She was very hospitable, and invited many relations and other guests to stay at Windsor, and liked to show them all over the castle, even into the kitchen.

The Queen's first public appearance of importance was when, the month after her accession, she dissolved Parliament, and herself read her speech from the throne. Her voice was said to be exquisite, and her manner of speaking quite perfect. Next year came her coronation. She seems to have enjoyed the great day immensely. As she drove through the enthusiastic crowds on her way to Westminster Abbey, she felt proud to be the Queen of such a nation. When she got back to the palace, ten hours after she had set out, she did not really feel tired, and after dinner felt much gratified when Lord Melbourne said to her, with tears in his eyes, "You did it beautifully—every part of it with so much taste." Later, from her mother's balcony, she watched the fireworks.

The idea of her marriage with Prince Albert was still cherished; but she was in no hurry, and meanwhile was very anxious about his education. She wrote to her uncle that it was her great desire to see "Albert a very good and distinguished young man." In 1839 he again visited England with his brother, and it was not long before the two young people fell genuinely in love with one another. It was the Queen who had to make the proposal. She called him to her room and, feeling it a very nervous moment, told him of her wish. She wrote to her uncle: "The warm affection he showed me on learning this gave me great pleasure.... I love him more than I can say.... I do feel very, very happy." They were married the following February, and the Queen found in Prince Albert all the happiness she had hoped for. In after years when she looked back, she felt that the years of her reign before their marriage were the least sensible and satisfactory parts of her whole life, "because of the constant amusement and flattery and mere politics" in which she had lived. Now she had the joy of a companion to help her in all her work and to share her life with her. But at first there were difficulties. Prince Albert was not popular; he was too German for English people to understand him. The Queen bitterly resented the attacks made on him. The ministers did not like him to take any part in affairs, and his position was very uncomfortable. But in time he showed how much he could help the Queen, and came to share all her work. They had nine children, and the Queen was a devoted mother, so it was well that she had the prince's help in her public life. Her love and admiration for him were unbounded. After three years of married life, she wrote to her uncle: "I am grateful for possessing (really without vanity or flattery or blindness) the most perfect being as a husband in existence, or who ever did exist; and I doubt whether anybody ever did love or respect another as I do my dear angel."

The Marriage of Queen Victoria to H.R.H. Prince Albert. (From the Picture by Sir George Hayter at Windsor Castle.)

In 1842 they paid their first visit to Scotland, and enjoyed it immensely. So much did the Queen love the quiet and liberty of her life in Scotland, that after several visits she rented Balmoral House in Aberdeenshire that she might have a Scotch home of her own; and after a while was able to buy the estate and build a new house on it. She did not like London after her marriage, and wanted a place where she and her family could live undisturbed by too many officials, so she also bought a place in the Isle of Wight and built Osborne House there. At both Osborne and Balmoral life was very simple. The Queen would run in and out of the house as she liked, and walked about alone, visiting the cottagers and enjoying her talks with them.

The Queen and Prince Albert gave much attention to the education of their children. Lady Lyttelton was named royal governess and superintended the nursery. The children were brought up very simply; the Queen spent as much time as she could with them, played with them, and interested herself in their friends and their pets, and they were encouraged to act little plays and recite poetry to their parents. Prince Albert, like the Queen, was very musical, and they often sang together. When the famous composer, Mendelssohn, visited England, he was invited to Buckingham Palace, and they both sang to his accompaniment. He said that the Queen sang "really quite faultlessly and with charming feeling and expression." They also loved the theatre, and plays were often acted at Windsor.

Several times the Queen visited Germany with Prince Albert, and they also went to Ireland. But wherever they were they never failed in their attention to public business. It was a great grief to the Queen when a change in the government came, and Lord Melbourne had to resign. But she always remained friends with him and wrote to him constantly. At first she dreaded having to do with his successor, Sir Robert Peel, but she grew to like and admire him very much. With nearly all her ministers her relations were most cordial; only with Lord Palmerston did she find it difficult to get on, and she never was quite easy with Gladstone. They all alike admired her industry and strong sense of duty, and her great knowledge of public affairs.

Lord Palmerston. From a seated figure in Hayter's Reformed Parliament in the National Portrait Gallery.

In 1851 the first International Exhibition was held in London. The idea of such an exhibition was Prince Albert's, and at first it met with great opposition, both at home and abroad. But it turned out a triumphant success. Many foreign princes came to the opening ceremony. The Queen described it to her uncle as "the greatest day in our history, the most beautiful and imposing and touching spectacle ever seen, and the triumph of my beloved Albert." People hoped that this great gathering of all nations would prove a festival of peace. But it was only a very few years afterwards that the Crimean War broke out. In this war England took part as the ally of Napoleon III. who had just made himself Emperor of France. The Queen followed the war with the deepest anxiety. She felt proud of the conduct of her troops, as she always called them; she welcomed them on their return, presented them with medals with her own hands, and did all in her power to show sympathy with their sufferings. Before the war was over, she paid her first visit to Paris to show her friendship for the Emperor, whose personal charm at that time attracted her very much; later she learnt to distrust him. She was received with immense enthusiasm, and wrote that she was "delighted, enchanted, amused, and interested, and had never seen anything more beautiful and gay than Paris."

William Ewart Gladstone.

When the Crimean War was over, the Queen visited Aldershot, and reviewed the troops herself. She started a new order, called the Victoria Cross, to be given to those soldiers who had done some specially brave act, and gave it herself to fifty-two men at a review in Hyde Park.

In 1856 her eldest daughter was betrothed to the Crown Prince of Prussia. The Queen was delighted, and showed her high spirits by dancing vigorously at all the balls given in honour of the betrothal. She even danced a Scottish reel to the bagpipes. The next year came the great anxiety of the Indian mutiny. The Queen felt it much more distressing than the Crimean War, "where there was glory and honourable warfare, and where the poor women and children were safe." It was also a sorrow to part from her eldest daughter when she married, but she rejoiced in her happiness and visited her in Germany. In 1859, at the age of thirty-nine, she became a grandmother when her first grandchild, the present Emperor of Germany, was born. Her family were an ever-growing joy to her, and life was full or interest and happiness.

The Victoria Cross. Instituted in 1856.

But in the year 1861 a sudden end came to her happiness. In the spring her mother died; and she wrote as a broken-hearted child to her uncle, saying that she could not imagine life without her. A greater blow was awaiting her. Before the end of the year, Prince Albert fell ill, and, almost before his illness was known to be serious, he died. The Queen was utterly crushed. In her first broken-hearted letter to her uncle, she said: "My life as a happy one is ended, the world is gone for me." It was indeed a terrible loss for her. She had absolutely depended on him and leant on his advice, and she had loved him and looked up to him as a perfect being. Ten years before, she had written about his wonderful fitness for business and politics, and added: "I grow daily to dislike them both, more and more. We women are not made for governing—and if we are good women, we must dislike these masculine occupations." Now she was left to govern alone, bereft of what had been the joy of her home life. Immense sympathy was shown to her and she was much touched by it. She determined to take her husband's example as her guide, and to give the same minute care as he had given to public affairs. But she shut herself up in absolute seclusion, seeing no one but her family and those whom she had to see for business.

Marriage of H.R.H. Victoria, Princess Royal, to H.R.H. Prince Frederick William of Prussia. (From the Picture by John Philip at Windsor Castle.)

At first, people accepted the Queen's seclusion as natural and respected her grief. But as the years passed and she made no change, many complaints were made of her neglect of the duties of her position. The newspapers published criticisms of her conduct, which deeply wounded her. She made no change, and spoke of herself as a cruelly misunderstood woman. At first, her only public appearances were to unveil statues of her husband, and occasionally she opened Parliament. She worked as hard as ever at public business, and was much taken up with family affairs and with the arrangements for the marriage of her children. She liked best to be at Balmoral, and felt Windsor a sad and gloomy place. During these years her seclusion led to her being decidedly unpopular, and it may rightly be considered the one serious mistake in her life.

The serious illness of the Prince of Wales in 1871 roused much sympathy and helped to make the Crown again more popular. When Mr. Disraeli became Prime Minister the Queen began to find public business more interesting. He was not only clever, but he took much trouble to be agreeable to her and to amuse her, so that she became really fond of him. She was delighted with his Indian policy, which ended in her being proclaimed Empress of India in 1876. She much enjoyed this new honour, and showed her feeling for India by having Indian servants to attend upon her, and by beginning to learn Hindustani.

Benjamin Disraeli, Lord Beaconsfield.

As the years passed, many sorrows came to the Queen through the death of relations and friends; especially she felt the death of her second daughter, Princess Alice. She continued to exert much influence on public affairs, and always did all in her power to help to keep the peace in Europe. In 1879 she visited Italy for the first time, and she often repeated her visit and travelled also in other countries, always in a very quiet and simple way.

In 1887 the Queen had been on the throne for fifty years, and she was persuaded to keep her Jubilee publicly. On the Jubilee Day, June 21, 1887, she went in procession, preceded by thirty-two princes of her own family, sons, sons-in-law, and grandsons, to a thanksgiving service in Westminster Abbey. Representatives of all the countries of Europe, of India, and the colonies followed her. The immense crowds who gathered to see her pass received her with an enthusiasm which deeply touched her. She said on her return to Buckingham Palace that she was very tired but very happy. The same enthusiasm attended other celebrations in connection with the Jubilee. In her old age the Queen was as popular, perhaps even more popular, than she had been in her youth. People in all the wide lands which made up the British Empire felt that she was the outward sign of the unity of the Empire. They venerated her for her long and blameless life, devoted to duty. In far distant lands, black and savage people honoured the great white Queen and trusted in her justice.

Photo: London Stereoscopic Co. Queen Victoria's Jubilee, 1897.

After the Jubilee, she went about a little more and saw more people; she visited Berlin, and spent some time in the south of Europe each year. She received many royal visitors, and once more there were concerts and dramatic performances at court. In spite of her age she still gave as much attention as ever to business, and would spend two or three hours a day going through papers, and signing her name to public documents.

In 1897 when she had reigned sixty years, her second, or diamond, Jubilee was celebrated. This

260

time a great state procession was made all through London, and on reaching St. Paul's Cathedral, the Queen's carriage paused at the bottom of the steps for a brief service of thanksgiving.

Her last years were clouded by the war in South Africa. Amidst all the gloom that followed on the news of the disasters suffered there by the English troops, the Queen never despaired of ultimate success. She took every opportunity of showing her sympathy with her soldiers, and telling them of her gratitude for their exertions. The war was not over when she began to show signs of failing health. One of the last things she did was to receive Lord Roberts to hear from him about the state of things in Africa. Little more than a week afterwards she died, at the age of eighty-one.

When we think over her long life and the great position she filled, we find that she owed her influence more to the strong sense of duty she always had, and to her constant determination to do what she felt to be right, than to any special gifts or talents she possessed. She was a wonderful woman because she was always true to the best that she knew, and it is this that makes her an example for us all.

www.ingramcontent.com/pod-product-compliance
Lightning Source LLC
Chambersburg PA
CBHW031933090426
42811CB00002B/170